Peter Earle was educated at University College, London, and
the London School of Economics. He became a lecturer in
economic history at the London School of Economics in 1964.
He has contributed several articles to the *History of the English
Speaking Peoples*, *History Makers* and to various learned journals.
His previous publications include *The Life and Times of James II*
(in the Kings and Queens series), *Corsairs of Malta and Barbary*
and a biography of Robert E. Lee. He is at present working on
a life of Daniel Defoe.

THE LIFE AND TIMES OF HENRY V

Peter Earle

Introduction by Antonia Fraser

CARDINAL edition published in 1975
by Sphere Books Ltd
30/32 Gray's Inn Road, London WC1X 8JL

First published in Great Britain by
Weidenfeld & Nicolson and Book Club Associates 1972
Copyright © George Weidenfeld & Nicolson and
Book Club Associates 1972

Set in Linotype Lectura

Printed in Great Britain by
Hazell Watson & Viney Ltd
Aylesbury, Bucks

CONTENTS

ACKNOWLEDGMENTS

Photographs and illustrations were supplied by, or are reproduced by kind permission of the following. Bibliothèque Arsenal, plate 41; Bodleian Library, Oxford, plates 3, 4, 22; British Museum, plates I, II, III, IV, V, VI, X, 1, 7, 8, 10, 11, 12, 13, 15, 16, 17, 19, 29, 31, 37, 38, 43, 44, 46, 47, 48, 49, 50; Bulloz, plate 36; Dean and Chapter, Canterbury, plates 20, 24; Courtauld Institute, plates 51, 52, 53; Department of the Environment, plate 2; Entwhistle Photographic Services, plate 24; Fitzwilliam Museum, Cambridge, plate 30; Photographie Giraudon, plates 25, 33, 42; Jarrold's, Norwich, plate 54; Kunsthistorisches Museum, Vienna, plate 40; Lambeth Palace Library, plate VIII, Louvre, Paris, plate 42; Mansell Collection, plate 39; Musée Condé, Chantilly, plate VII; Musée Jacquemart-André, plate 36; National Gallery, plate 9; National Portrait Gallery, plate IX; National Monuments Record, plates 14, 20; Public Records Office, plates 34, 45; Receuil d'Arras, plate 25; Thomas Photos, Oxford, plate 26; Victoria and Albert Museum, plates 5, 6, 21, 23, 35; Dean and Chapter of Westminster, plates 27, 28, 54.

INTRODUCTION

Henry v, Shakespeare's martial King, occupies a central position in all our historical imaginations. It would be hard indeed to picture his reign without conjuring up the ghost not only of 'warlike Harry' but also of that boon companion of his youth, the immortal Falstaff, or the famous Percy – 'this Hotspur in swathing clothes, this infant warrior'. Yet just as our concepts of the King are captured unforgettably by the militant poetry with which Shakespeare clothes his hero's story, so too Henry's own life is too much dominated – in popular terms – by the single victory for which he is so much renowned: that of Agincourt in October 1415.

A real biography of Henry begins by correcting certain of Shakespeare's impressions (Hotspur was in fact considerably older than Henry and at one point his guardian) and confirming others: the legend of the youthful dissipation, in 'the service of Venus as well as Mars' as one chronicler put it, seems well-founded, as is the subsequent recantation and steady adherence to the more sober paths of kingship. But Henry in truth reflects far more facets of English medieval history than the mere necessity for winning battles. Born far removed from the succession to the throne, a great-grandson of Edward III, by his twelfth birthday he had become the next heir. Nothing could illustrate the see-saws of the late fourteenth century more effectively than the rise of Henry's father Bolingbroke, later Henry IV, who, on the basis of landed power built up by his own father John of Gaunt, proved that a magnate could successfully challenge the rightful royal line.

The demotion of the Plantagenets and the succession of his own Lancastrian father, combined with the quelling of subsequent risings against the new King, emphasised to the young Henry what he can never have seriously doubted within the climate of his own times: the essential skill at arms of a young knight was to be directed towards general aggrandisement of the royal sphere of influence, and the determined pursuit of any rights not yet pressed home. Thus Henry v's French Wars, which occupied so much of his nine-year reign and were still unresolved at his early death in 1422 at the age of thirty-five, inevitably pushed forward the Plantagenet claim to the French throne. As Peter Earle brilliantly demonstrates by building up a character study of Henry with much emphasis on his youth and upbringing, Henry's 'pursuit of dynastic knight-errantry' might well be out of date, and it might well have been far more beneficial to his country to have stayed at home: nevertheless it would have been a strange solution for 'a man brought up to fight' as Henry had undoubtedly been. As a result, Agincourt, the greatest triumph of a medieval warrior who heard mass before battle, wore the unmistakable royal surcoat disdainful of personal danger, and distinguished himself in combat in the course of the conflict, becomes the supreme illustration of a fifteenth-century King's career, not its solitary known feature.

Antonia Fraser

I

A Noble Education 1387–99

Once upon a time there was a king who won a battle. After half a millennium the reputation of Henry V still rests squarely on the events of one day in late October 1415. One day spent fighting in the middle of a very large cornfield halfway between Boulogne and Arras. The field of Agincourt looks today much as it must have done then and, although it is a pretty and peaceful place, it is not difficult to imagine the battle. Stand on the country road between the villages of Agincourt and Tramecourt and look to the north across the young wheat. This must be almost exactly on the line held by the English as they awaited the onslaught of the enormous French army. If they had turned and run, Henry V would have been just another rather unsuccessful medieval king. Because the English knights and archers held the line and won the battle he became 'that princely hero who, through the splendour of his achievements, illumined with the rays of his glory the decline of the medieval world'. Such is fame.

The hero of Agincourt reigned for only nine years and died at the age of thirty-five, 'too famous to live long'. The story of the first third of his life is virtually unknown to us. His birth passed unrecorded by the heavenly hosts; there were no thunderbolts, no eclipse of the sun, not even a two-headed calf to astonish the world on such an eventful day. Indeed the day itself is unknown. Henry was not born to be king, and there is no mention of the event in the chronicles of the times. It has been left to the ingenuity of historians to establish that Henry of Monmouth was born in the gatehouse tower of Monmouth Castle in the late summer of 1387.

The birth of a boy who was to become one of England's most glorious and admired kings was for his mother just the beginning of her martyrdom for the principles of dynasticism. Married at the age of ten, Mary de Bohun was seventeen when she gave birth to Henry.

Three sons and two daughters later she died in childbirth at the age of twenty-four. The children must have missed their gay young mother who loved to sing to the lute and ride with her hounds. Maybe her husband did too. At any rate her duty had been done, and no doubt on his rare visits to her household Bolingbroke was proud of her. For Mary, once destined for the convent, had brought him many titles, including the earldoms of Hereford, Essex and Northampton, and half the enormous estates which the Norman De Bohuns had so patiently built up since the Conquest. Furthermore she had insured against that greatest catastrophe of a great family, the failure of heirs. All four of Mary's boys were healthy and survived to manhood, and all four were to make their mark on history.

Mary's husband, Henry of Bolingbroke, Earl of Derby, was not present at the birth of his eldest son and heir. Man of action, traveller and soldier, his time was spent in almost constant movement, from castle to castle, country to country, camp to camp. The winter and spring of 1386–7, in the early months of Mary's pregnancy, had been particularly busy. For Bolingbroke, like the rest of his class, had been preparing to resist a full-scale invasion from the traditional enemy across the Channel. After half a century of intermittent warfare, nearly all carried out on their own territory, the French were preparing a massive counterstroke. All through the summer of 1385 and the winter of 1386–7 ships, men and supplies were being concentrated in the Norman ports. The feverish activity of the French was matched in England, and Bolingbroke himself contracted to serve his King and defend his country with some two thousand men of his own retinue. But time passed, the French lost their nerve, and slowly drifted away from the Channel ports back to the safety of their homes. The danger was over. England could rest, and Bolingbroke could make his way to Monmouth to greet his heir, the very prince who thirty years later would show the French how a conquest should be managed. But Bolingbroke did not stay long. A few weeks of domestic bliss, a few games of chess with his young wife and then he was off again. This time, together with other great lords, he was fighting the soldiers of his own King, Richard II, in an attempt to curb the growing absolute power of the King and his favourites. The victory of the Lords Appellant – Bolingbroke, the Duke of Gloucester and the earls of Arundel, Warwick and Nottingham – at the battle of Radcot Bridge, and the subsequent bloody destruction of the King's favourites ushered in one of the few quiet periods in the turbulent reign of Richard II. But revenge for the success of Bolingbroke and the other four Lords Appellant was to dominate Richard's policy in the last years of his reign.

Henry of Bolingbroke was the eldest son of John of Gaunt, Duke of Lancaster, the fourth son of Edward III. When he was nineteen John of Gaunt had been married to the co-heiress of the House of Lancaster, his cousin Blanche. Half the estates of such a House was no mean dowry for an ambitious youth, but when his wife's sister died the following year, he found himself possessed of the whole magnificent inheritance, no doubt some compensation for his grief. John of Gaunt, as befitted a King's son, was now a magnate, a member of that group of about a dozen noble families whose estates and power were so great that they dominated the politics of England during the later Middle Ages.

The power of a magnate was firmly founded in landed wealth and it was his first duty and desire to increase his inheritance; that is, to increase his estates. For the arithmetic of power was simple. More land meant more money, more money meant more castles and more men pledged to your service. Money and men meant power and glory. Power meant many things, but at the very simplest it meant the power to acquire even more land. As a result we find that, barring accidents, the lands and power of the magnates were growing in a cumulative way in the fourteenth century. The methods of increasing an inheritance were numerous. Estates could be bought, maybe out of money won in war, a favourite occupation of this class. Estates could be married. But the most lucrative and also the most risky way of increasing an inheritance was through the seeking of royal favour. Royal favour could be won in many ways. It was, as we have seen, an advantage to be the son of a king. It would help to win a battle for the King, or at least to show oneself a distinguished commander in the field. It made good sense to be on the right side in a civil war. The beginnings of the Lancastrian inheritance came from the confiscated estates of Simon de Montfort after his defeat at Evesham by the future Edward I. But perhaps the commonest way of acquiring royal favour was through successful manoeuvring in the royal court. If the game of the court could be played by the new man seeking to place his family on the map, it could also be played by the established magnate. But for everyone it was a nerve-wracking game which required much skill and endurance. As a Frenchman put it: 'the Court is an assembly of people who, under the pretence of acting for the good of all, come together to diddle each other; for there's scarcely anyone who is not engaged in buying and selling and exchanging, sometimes their income, sometimes their old clothes – for we of the court are high-class merchants, we buy the other people – and sometimes for their money we sell *them* our own precious humanity'. The rewards for those who could win at this game were enormous, and a magnate was more likely to win than anyone else, for fortune normally favours those already fortunate. In the King's gift were confiscated estates, and others which had returned to the Crown through failure of heirs, pensions, offices and marriages to heiresses. But what the King gave he could take away, and much of the history of the reign of Richard II is concerned with the King giving and taking away, as he strove to replace the power of the magnates by his own absolute rule.

In the league of magnates there was no doubt who was the leader. The fortunes of the House of Lancaster had been pushed forward by a series of distinguished and capable men using every one of the methods mentioned above. By the time of Henry's birth, his grandfather, John of Gaunt, had built Lancaster up into a power nearly equal to that of King Richard himself. The outward and visible signs of this power were everywhere: some thirty castles, scattered over the length and breadth of the kingdom, but mainly in Yorkshire, the Midlands and South Wales; the ability to put 1,000 men-at-arms and 3,000 archers into the field for Richard's expedition to Scotland in 1385, half as many again as the royal levies and five times as many as the retinue of the next most powerful nobleman; an income sufficient to make any king jealous. Such power could present a great threat to the King, or it could be a great support. In the 1380s there was much suspicion of John of Gaunt's ambitions. But by the early 1390s, as Henry grew up, it seemed that Lancaster was now a prop to the Crown. Bolingbroke was back in favour, and John of Gaunt was the King's most loyal supporter. As Richard once again developed his liking for absolute power, he must have looked with suspicion at the power of his uncle and cousin, and of their potential allies among the great. But for the time being all was peaceful between Richard and the House of Lancaster.

It was, then, in this environment, as the heir of Henry of Boling-broke, the heir of John of Gaunt, that Henry of Monmouth grew up. Little is known of his childhood, but it is clear that he lived the normal life of a young nobleman and received the normal education of his class. What did this consist of? One of the most striking aspects of the nobleman's life was his constant movement. The estates and castles of a magnate were nearly always widely scattered, and much of his life was spent just moving about from one castle to another. Though he might well have a favourite residence, his power rested largely on the loyalty of his tenants and retainers, and unless such people saw him from time to time they might soon forget just how powerful and magnificent he was. The progress of a magnate about the country was a laborious and impressive undertaking. For reasons both of safety and show a great man would always have a large retinue when he travelled. This might run to several hundreds of soldiers and servants, their numbers often swollen by lesser men quick to seek a great lord's protection on the dangerous roads, for England was a lawless place. Ahead of the great man would go an advance party with heralds; behind him would follow his baggage, scores of carts loaded with food, fuel, harness, household utensils, and wine, maybe with some of his precious furnishings, his tapestries, even his windows, to be hung in each castle where he stayed.

These castles were changing with the times. Though they still retained their defensive function, greater wealth and greater splendour were converting them from draughty and uncomfortable keeps into magnificent palaces. Entering through a great gatehouse, itself often palatial in its interior, one now saw buildings all round the inner courtyard protected by its curtain wall. On one side would be the quarters of the lord, on the other the stables and the lodgings of his retainers. Often there was no way within between the two groups of buildings, for many lords feared their retainers as much as they depended on them. The main feature of the lord's quarters would be his great hall giving access at one end to the kitchen and buttery, and at the other to his private apartments. Both hall and apartments were growing in comfort and magnificence with wall-paintings, costly furnishings and hangings, the emphasis being more and more on comfort and light, sometimes at the expense of defence. Of all the castle builders and improvers of the second half of the fourteenth century no one was the equal of John of Gaunt. He lavished money on Lancaster itself, Tutbury, Dunstanburgh and in particular Kenilworth, his favourite castle, whose great banqueting hall was reckoned the finest in the country after Westminster.

The hall, often retaining its central hearth, was the centre of castle life. Here the lord held his court, a royal court in miniature, some-times imitating the advanced fashions of the royal court, sometimes old-fashioned and indeed deliberately archaic. Here, while the lord was in residence, was the setting-place for great feasts, for entertainments, minstrels, mummers, dancing, recitation and performing bears. But there was much entertainment out of doors as well: jousting, the sport of a military caste, falconry, and especially the chase, for 'of hunting there is no season of all the year, that game may not be found in every good country, also hounds ready to chase it'. In the midst of this constant round of entertainment, the lord found time to administer his estates, or at least to hear the reports of his stewards and bailiffs, to indulge in politics, to patch up old alliances and make new ones. It was a busy but quite attractive life.

Merely to grow up in a world like this was an education, and often the young nobleman received little more. The sons of the nobility very rarely went to school. As young children their care was left to the women of the household, and later to the male servants. Sometimes a tutor would be installed. At the age of eleven they might become a page to a friend of their father and learn how to behave as a young nobleman. At fourteen the real business of life would start, and they would become a squire and learn the skills of war preparatory to investiture as a knight. This, or something like it, was the education of the young Henry, though it is probable that his progress was more precocious.

As he travelled from castle to castle he would learn something of the geography of England. Talking to his father's and his grandfather's retainers he would learn something of the geography and politics of a wider world. The retainers of the House of Lancaster were well-travelled. Some had made the pilgrimage to the Holy Land and could tell him of the astonishing wealth of the merchant cities of Italy, of the deeds of the Crusaders, their ancestors, and of the present peril of Christian Europe as the Moslem Turks pushed ever further into the heart of Christendom. Some no doubt were present at the catastrophic battle of Nicopolis in 1396 when Turkish arms shattered the chivalry of Europe. Others could tell him of his father's exploits against the heathen Lithuanians and Letts, or of his grandfather's expeditions into Spain. And nearly all could tell him first hand of France. He would learn of the English King's claim to the Crown of France, and of the great wars that had been fought to enforce that claim in the last half-century. The name and glory of Crécy and Poitiers would be familiar, told to him by old men who had fought there. Of more recent vintage he would hear of his grandfather's great raid from Calais to Bordeaux in 1373–4. Many of these old soldiers might well miss the glory and plunder of the French wars, and speak with contempt of the truce recently signed by King Richard. Some of them were to fight alongside Henry when he renewed these wars in his turn. For the moment they were idle, maybe bored, though there were compensations. When Henry was three years old, bored knights from all over Europe, including his father, made their way to the field of St Inglevert near Calais to accept the challenge of a group of French knights that they would hold the field for thirty days against all comers.

A boy who liked tales, and there is no doubt that Henry was such a boy, would hear stories of a different kind of war, more glamorous perhaps than the English wars in France. For a constant diet in any place where young noblemen gathered was the tales of chivalry. It would take an intelligent boy to tell the difference between the adventures of Sir Galahad and the Black Prince – the ideal and the reality. Indeed, there seems no doubt that there was confusion in many a late medieval mind on this score. The ideals of chivalry fitted uneasily with the realities of the *chevauchée*, a journey of destruction which left the poor homeless and starving, towns burnt, women raped, churches plundered and no enemy on whom the rampaging knight might test his prowess. And yet these ideals still mattered, and to learn them was part of a nobleman's education. The cynical might scoff; many might secretly agree with the view of life attributed to Sir Dinadan in the French *Tristan*. 'Life to him was good, and its goodness was not likely to be enhanced by an artificial code of conduct. You fight only when you have to – a live coward is in reality better than a dead knight.' Despite the attractiveness of such a philosophy and the anachronism of several of the ideals of chivalry, many young knights still tried to live up to these ideals.

What were these ideals? There was first the practical virtue of skill at arms, but coupled with this was an admiration for audacity, for the man who 'did not value death at two cherries'. Equally important was the virtue of loyalty. It was the conflict between different loyalties that most often got the knight into trouble. For a knight owed loyalty to many men – to his family, his friends, his lord, his king and his Church, as well as to people with whom his relationship was more temporary, such as his host for the night. Who was to come first? One thing that seems quite clear is that his king was likely to come a long way down the list, while the concept of loyalty to one's country had hardly been developed at all. It was still a world where personal relationships were all important and the breaking of a pledged word the greatest social crime of all. Other virtues which were important for the knight were compassion and generosity — compassion for those who had been treated unjustly, generosity to the poor and to one's friends. Generosity implied a disdain for wealth, and a good knight must be without the desire to amass treasure and riches. Such virtues were difficult to find in a cruel and mercenary world. But many tried, even while their fellows viewed war and knighthood as a means to adventure and riches, and a Falstaff might remark that 'the better part of valour is discretion'. One who tried, quite consciously, to live the life of a noble knight was Henry's friend, Richard Beauchamp, Earl of Warwick. One of Henry's most trusted commanders in his French campaigns, he was a brave and chivalrous warrior who modelled his famous jousting exploits on the pattern of Arthurian romance. Henry, too, was well imbued with the ideals of chivalry. On many occasions in his adult life he was to carry out the most flamboyantly knightly deeds. But there is a certain sense of drama in Henry's rashness, skill at arms, compassion and generosity, just as there is in his much-vaunted piety. However genuine he may have been in reality, the image that comes down to us is one of a supremely successful showman who knew how to manipulate those characteristics most admired by his contemporaries to his own advantage. His generosity is matched by efficient collection of his share of prize-money, his compassion by his ruthless cruelty when it suited his purpose. His rashness is too well calculated to be rash. For Henry was imbued with another attribute much praised by the later medieval knight — he was wise. 'Be a man never so valiant nor so big yet he be overmatched . . . For manhood is not worth but if it be meddled with wisdom.'

One knightly virtue which Henry certainly acquired, and at an early age, was skill at arms. He fought in his first battle at the age of sixteen, and on that occasion and for the rest of his fighting life he was prominent as an individual as well as a leader. Many of these skills he no doubt learned in the field itself, but it is probable that he had learned to fight while still a boy. He certainly had a sword by the age of ten, and he would have had plenty of opportunity of practice in its

18

use with his father's retainers. By the same age he knew how to ride, swim and bend a bow, and just before his tenth birthday it is recorded that Henry was at a tournament at Pleshey Castle, in Essex, on his fine horse, its saddle covered in black silk. Another pastime which was considered to be an excellent school of arms and fieldcraft was the chase, and there is evidence that Henry was much addicted to hunting, and indeed was something of an expert at it. *The Master of Game*, a delightful book written by his rather shifty cousin, Edward, Duke of York, was dedicated to Prince Henry, for his 'noble and wise correction'. Here we learn that a good hunter should begin to learn his art at the age of seven or eight or a little older. Once learnt, nothing could be more delightful, or more pleasing to God, since the practice of hunting is so time-consuming that it leaves no time for idleness, from the morning, when the hunter rises and 'sees a sweet and fair morn and clear weather and bright, and he heareth the song of the small birds', till the evening when he returns home and washes his thighs and legs, 'and peradventure all his body', eats and drinks and is glad and well. In the meantime he has pitched his wits and his courage against the falseness and malice of the cat, the marvellous great cunning of the hart, or the boar who can 'slit a man from knee up to the breast and slay him all stark dead at one stroke so that he never spake thereafter'. What better training for a life-time of war?

But all this is to take a rather one-sided view of the education of a noble knight. While many knights were illiterate, Henry certainly was not, though his formal education was probably rather thin. Indeed he had little time to learn, for his boyhood stopped abruptly at the age of twelve, when he moved on to a stage where there was little opportunity for book-learning. Still, by that age, though he almost certainly never went to school, he had learned to read and write and had acquired the rudiments of education. What is more, he had as tutor for some at least of his childhood one of the most brilliant men of his time, his uncle Henry Beaufort. This precocious, scheming man, learned in theology and already wise in the ways of the world, was appointed Chancellor of Oxford in 1397, at the age of twenty, and Bishop of Lincoln at twenty-one. The talented Beaufort family, who were to play such an outstanding role in Henry's life, were the children of John of Gaunt by his mistress, Katherine Swynford. The open alliance and later marriage of the ageing Gaunt with this lady, formerly the governess to his daughters, had scandalised the court in the mid-90s, but all was forgiven, and the children of the alliance were legitimised in 1397. As a child Henry also acquired what was to be a life-long appreciation of music. By the age of ten he had a harp which he could probably play. Indeed to play on the harp and improvise songs was quite a common attribute of the nobility, and one which enabled them to appreciate the art of the minstrels who played such an important part in castle society.

One other feature of a medieval education needs to be discussed. The previous emphasis on worldly learning should not allow us to forget that the society into which Henry was born was intensely religious. Every lord had his chapel and his priest, and Henry from the earliest age would have received religious instruction from the ladies and priests of the household. A Benedictine monk who was close to Henry in his youth praises his punctuality in attending mass, his weekly confession and his habit, obviously not shared by all, of sitting out the service. Henry's piety and attendance to his religious duties were characteristics of his adult life that are mentioned by all commentators. But the Church, indeed the Christian world, of Henry's time was not in a particularly healthy state. Two Popes, at one time three, mocked the unity of the Church. Nearer home the Lollards ridiculed some of the fundamental doctrines of the Catholic faith, and preached a dangerous form of social criticism. And on the borders of Christendom the situation had never looked so dangerous as the Turks advanced. Christian chivalry had long lost its dominion in the Holy Land, and the Moslem counter-attack now stood on the borders of Hungary. All three of these problems were to worry Henry as a man, and he was to play an important part in attempting to solve them. Though he never lived to fulfil his dream of leading a Crusade against the Turks, he played a part in bringing about the end of the Papal Schism. And as for his local problem, both he and his father were noted for their persecution and burning of Lollards, to the horror of otherwise adulatory historians who saw in them the precursors of the Protestant Reformation. Henry was a good Catholic as a Christian knight should be. In theory, indeed, there should be no distinction between the worldly and spiritual endeavours of a knight. In practice there was a tendency to swing from excessive worldliness to excessive piety, and in Henry, as we have already seen, this tendency was likely to be exaggerated by his showmanship.

The pattern of Henry's childhood and education was rudely disturbed in 1398 when he was eleven years old. In the previous year King Richard had taken his revenge against the three eldest of the Lords Appellant who had so humiliated him ten years previously. The King's uncle, Gloucester, was murdered in Calais, the Earl of Warwick was sent to the Isle of Man in perpetual banishment, the Earl of Arundel was executed at Tower Hill, whilst his brother, Thomas Arundel, the Archbishop of Canterbury, was sentenced to perpetual banishment. It was now the turn of the other two, Bolingbroke and Thomas Mowbray. Both of them had recently been the recipients of the King's favour and they had been raised to the dukedoms of Hereford and Norfolk, but they must have been uneasy. Thomas Mowbray confided his uneasiness to Bolingbroke and the latter, on his father's advice, reported Mowbray's treasonable remarks to the King. Mowbray stoutly denied Bolingbroke's accusation of treason and, since there had been no witnesses to the conversation, it was decided that the truth could only be determined by trial by combat. For Richard it seemed a god-sent opportunity to get rid of the last two of his old enemies at one go. Elaborate preparations had been made for such an exciting contest and the battle was just about to begin, when Richard in the most dramatic way stopped the combat and exiled both the contestants, Bolingbroke for ten years and Mowbray for life. Henry was probably present at these famous Lists of Coventry, but what his thoughts were at the unexpected *dénouement* we do not know. For it is possible that his sympathies were not entirely on one side. The choice between allegiance to one's King and allegiance to one's father was just another of those cases of conflicting loyalties which troubled the life of a knight. In Henry's case it must have been a particularly difficult choice. For his father, still a great traveller, must have been something of a stranger to him, while Richard had already shown him much affection. As it turned out, Henry's ultimate loyalty was always to his father and the House of Lancaster, but he seems to have shown no repugnance when Richard retained him in his suite after his father's banishment. For the next year Henry completed his short education at the court of Richard II.

Richard's court must have been a fascinating place in the 1390s, despite its political undertones of rebellion and oppression. The whole style was rather different from previous English royal courts, and owed much to Continental example, partly through Richard's marriages into the royal families of Bohemia and France. Earlier English courts had tended to be geared to war; Richard's court was more peaceful, and though the knightly ideals remained, they tended to be more the ideals of the courtly knight than the knight in the field. There was an emphasis on intellectual and aesthetic activities. Poets, such as the ageing Chaucer, declaimed their own verse. Artists excelled, especially in the creation of minutely beautiful objects – jewellery, manuscript illuminations and tapestry work. Women, too, were much in evidence, and helped the court to create its own entertainment with new developments in music, dancing and song. Presiding over all was Richard, still quite a young man. As he continued to alienate the great of the land, he indulged his flamboyant tastes, and set each day a new fashion in magnificent dress. But above all the King, fascinated by the art of the kitchen, loved his food. His court cookery book has survived, and the recipes owe much to that trade in exotics which made the fortune of the Venetians. Minced pheasant with Greek wine, cinnamon, cloves, ginger and sugar; oysters in Greek wine; mulberries and honey – all washed down with the wines of France, Germany and the Mediterranean – were some of the dishes created to delight the court of Richard.

If Henry found all this a pleasant change from the baronial beef and venison of his earlier childhood, he did not have long to enjoy it. In February 1399 John of Gaunt died. In his last years he had been a loyal prop to Richard; as High Steward of England he had been in the forefront of the procedure which led to the destruction of the Lords Appellant, Gloucester, Arundel and Warwick, and when in turn his own son was banished he had said not a word. Gaunt's death would have been a good opportunity to pardon his son. Instead Richard took the step which was to lead to the rapid curtailment of his arbitrary exercise of power. Bolingbroke's exile was increased to life, and the King seized his inheritance. What the young Henry thought about this we do not know. That he behaved like the carefree child of a contemporary writer who wept more for the loss of an apple than of his heritage seems unlikely. What those magnates still in possession of their lands felt about the disinheritance of the House of Lancaster by a King becoming increasingly hysterical and monomaniac can easily be imagined. Who could now feel safe? And yet in the summer of the same year Richard, sublimely confident, set off to quell a rebellion in Ireland, the scene of one of his few triumphs. With him he took nearly all his supporters, leaving behind his last remaining uncle, the incompetent Edmund of York, as keeper of the realm. With him too he took the young Lord Henry.

A few weeks later Bolingbroke sailed from Boulogne for kingless England to claim his inheritance. As he made his triumphal march from

Ravenspur on the Humber across the middle of England to Bristol all resistance disappeared. His passage was studded with Lancastrian castles who threw their gates open at his approach. His small numbers were swollen by the retinues of great lords eager to greet and support him. The appearance of so many Lancastrians, Nevilles and Percies soon convinced the Duke of York of the folly of resistance; the royal army melted away. Richard's Cheshire archers, whose arrogance and depredations had been the prop of his power, slunk off to their homes, stripping off those 'white hart badges whose bestowal had lost the King so many faithful hearts'. Richard himself, whose personal courage had never been in doubt, deposited young Henry in the castle of Trim and left for the region in which he had most personal support, North Wales. It was a hopeless mission. Betrayed and deserted he soon found himself a prisoner of Bolingbroke in the Tower, later to be removed to the fatal safety of Lancastrian Pontefract, whilst his cousin considered what was to be done with him. That cousin, like a true Lancastrian, had found time to raise his sights during his march across England. Lancaster might be a fine inheritance, but how much finer was the Crown of England. Three months were sufficient to convert the exile in Boulogne into a king, three months to challenge successfully the Realm and Crown of England with the help of his kin and his friends, 'which Realm was in point to be undone for default of governance and undoing of the good laws'.

On hearing of Bolingbroke's invasion, Richard is reputed to have said to his enemy's son: 'Henry, my boy, see what thy father hath done to me.' In reply Henry pleaded his innocence of his father's deeds. There is no reason to doubt the truth of this, since it seems unlikely that Bolingbroke would have made a confidant of a son who was in the power of his rival. But the deed done, Bolingbroke, now Henry IV, made haste to implicate his children in the Lancastrian usurpation, and there is no evidence that they regretted it, or indeed that they shared the guilty conscience that was to haunt their father for the rest of his life. As soon as he was King, he sent a sea-captain to recall his eldest son from the castle of Trim. On 12 October he knighted his sons, disregarding the fact that Henry had already been knighted by Richard in Ireland. Next day Henry carried the sword of justice at his father's coronation, a celebration whose sanctity was increased by the use of a miraculous phial of oil, said to have been presented to St Thomas à Becket by the Virgin Mary and afterwards hidden at Poitiers, where it

23

had been found by Bolingbroke's grandfather. Immediately after the coronation it was announced that Henry was to be created Prince of Wales, Duke of Cornwall and Earl of Chester, and in early November he was duly invested with all these titles, plus the duchy of Aquitaine. As the new King and his children retired to Windsor Castle to celebrate Christmas they must have been a little exhausted by all the excitement. Perhaps the King was thinking of a bold remark that he had made at his coronation. When his champion had offered to do battle with anyone who challenged the King's title, Henry IV had said that he would defend his Crown in person if necessary. It was going to be necessary sooner than he thought.

2

The Struggle for the Crown 1399–1408

To seize the crown from an anointed king was a serious matter. Although the Plantagenets did not consider themselves quite as divine as did the Stuarts, there was at least a semi-holiness about a king, even a king whose crimes, according to the chronicler Adam of Usk, included 'perjuries, sacrileges, unnatural crimes, exactions from his subjects, reduction of his people to slavery, cowardice and weakness of rule'. Furthermore, although the English felt that there was some limit to what a king could do, unlike the French whose king had no other control over him 'than the fear of God and his own conscience', there was a strong belief in strict succession. Even if Richard deserved to be deposed, Henry was not his heir. The natural successor to the childless Richard should have been the Earl of March, an eight-year-old boy whose father had been killed in that unfortunate rebellion in Ireland which had drawn Richard out of his kingdom at such a critical time. So Henry was doubly a usurper, and owed his throne to his own power and ability, and the support of his friends. But a holy office once besmirched by usurpation is no longer holy, and Henry's example was to raise the sights of other noble houses in the century that followed his accession to the throne. In the meantime it was to be nine years before that throne could be considered safe as Scotsmen, Welshmen and English noble houses struggled to unseat him. During this 'scrambling and unquiet time' Prince Henry was one of the strongest props of his father, despite his extreme youth, and he was to be well and truly blooded in the cause of the House of Lancaster.

Indeed, his father relied very heavily on his immediate family. Henry's younger brothers were all given important and responsible jobs to do in their 'teens. Even more important was the support of the three

Beauforts, Henry IV's half-brothers, all of them talented men. Outside this small circle the new King could rely on the support of the knights, squires and clerks of the duchy of Lancaster, and it was these servants who supplied the bulk of administrative and military service to the King in the early years of his reign. Outside Lancaster Henry's allies were of necessity more doubtful. Most of the great noble and baronial houses supported his usurpation, but might become jealous and ambitious as his power and strength grew. His most distinguished supporter was Thomas Arundel, Archbishop of Canterbury, banished by Richard for his part in the actions of the Lords Appellant and immediately reinstated by Henry. Amongst other great men consistently loyal to the House of Lancaster it will suffice to mention the Archbishop's nephew, the Earl of Arundel, son of the man executed by Richard in 1397, the Beauchamps, Earls of Warwick, and the Nevilles, Earls of Westmorland. At the beginning of the reign one should add the powerful northern House of Percy to this list. The Percies' star had been in the ascendant in the fourteenth century, and they now stood very high in the league of magnates, and could rely on massive military support for any venture which they undertook. At this period they saw themselves as kingmakers, and it was their allegiance which had made Henry's adventure sure of success. They were led by three distinguished military commanders, Henry Percy, Earl of Northumberland, his brother Thomas, Earl of Worcester, and his son the famous Hotspur. Another family who saw themselves as kingmakers and whose allegiance was therefore doubtful, since kingmakers do not normally like strong kings, was the Mortimers, marcher lords of South Wales. The nominal head of this family was the eight-year-old Earl of March, whom Henry held securely in a fairly pleasant confinement, but the real head was the boy's uncle, Sir Edmund Mortimer. A family who never seem to have quite made up their mind whose side they were on was the House of York. We have already seen how Edmund of Langley rather feebly gave up at the appearance of Bolingbroke's army in 1399. His son, Edward, who had been much favoured by Richard, seems to have been a very shifty man who was lucky to live long enough to die gloriously at Agincourt. To close this survey of the noble field at the beginning of Henry's reign we must mention those who were quite definitely his enemies. For the most part these were the courtiers who had done best out of Richard's drive to personal rule. Most important were the Hollands and the Earl of Salisbury. John Holland, Duke of Exeter and

Earl of Huntingdon, was the son of Richard II's mother, Joan the 'Fair Maid of Kent', by her previous marriage with Sir Thomas Holland. He was therefore Richard's half-brother. His nephew Thomas, Duke of Surrey and Earl of Kent, also enjoyed the favour of King Richard. John Montacute, 3rd Earl of Salisbury, was an interesting character – pro-Lollard, pro-French and a minor poet of some reputation. He was a particular enemy of Bolingbroke, both because of his religious and political views and because he had been selected by King Richard as his personal agent in preventing Bolingbroke making an extremely favour-able second marriage while in exile in France. With the exception of Salisbury Henry's policy towards these men was to strip them of some of their lands and titles, but otherwise to treat them mercifully.

It turned out to be an unwise policy. As Henry and his family settled down to enjoy their first Christmas holiday at Windsor Castle, details of a plot to kill them all and restore Richard to the throne were betrayed by one of the plotters, Edward, Earl of Rutland, the son of the Duke of York. The main conspirators were those Ricardian courtiers, led by the Hollands and the Earl of Salisbury, mentioned above. They had planned to smuggle armed men into the castle under cover of a tournament which Henry was holding on Twelfth Night. Warned just in time, Henry had no choice but to flee with his sons, and they rode fast for London as night drew on. Retribution followed fast after this undignified and, for the children at least, terrifying flight. Henry raised an army in London and set out to destroy his opponents, but there was no need. Richard's courtiers, much hated and blamed for many of the exactions of the last reign, were captured and lynched in various unpleasant ways by the common people. The plot made one thing clear. Richard was too dangerous to live. As long as he remained alive his person would be a rallying point for Henry's opponents. But Henry was not strong enough to execute an anointed king in the full glare of publicity. So, almost certainly at Henry's orders, Richard died in Pontefract Castle, secretly and shamefully, and Henry was for the rest of his life haunted by guilt and doubt – guilt for the murder of an anointed king, and doubt on the part of interested persons that Richard was really dead. King Richard is alive and in Scotland or Wales was a common claim, and one which Henry's opponents exploited cleverly, even producing a man who was Richard's double to fool the doubters.

The rebellion of the Earls was but a foretaste of the future. Henry was to be constantly on the move damping down the flames of revolt and aggression for the next few years. In the summer of 1400 he marched against Scotland, where border raiding had been intensified since his accession. With him went the young Prince Henry. Despite a few weeks burning and raiding with the Percies on the Scottish borders, it was a frustrating and rather humiliating expedition, so to be told on his way back south that the Welsh were in revolt must have been hard to bear, but hardly surprising. For 'the Welsh habit of revolt against the English is an old-standing madness' and Wales was one of the main areas of Ricardian sympathy. As the young Prince of Wales listened to the news, he must have reflected that his job was, after all, going to be no sinecure, but no one could have guessed that the Welsh would still be in revolt eight years later. They were eight years' education for a fighting king.

The part of Wales which belonged to Henry as Prince, the principality, was quite small and consisted mainly of the extreme west of the country. Between the principality and England lay the Welsh marches which were ruled almost as independent kingdoms by the marcher-lords, warrior barons such as the Talbots, Charltons, Greys and Mortimers. There was little love lost between these aggressive men in their powerful castles and the native Welsh whose natural instincts for dislike of English rule, English taxes and English law were fostered by the bards with tales of a glorious past and prophecies of a glorious future. But it should not be thought that the Welsh were all barefoot tribesmen clustered at the foot of baronial castles. The century of comparative peace since Edward I's conquest had given rise to a class of Welshmen who appeared to have forgotten their princely ancestors and were prepared to make the best of English rule. Living mainly in the principality, these well-educated and fairly wealthy Welsh country gentlemen formed a strong contrast to the warlike English barons, their neighbours. It was a niggling squabble between representatives of these two groups over the ownership of a piece of land that sparked off the last great Welsh rebellion.

Owen Glendower was about fifty years old at the beginning of the revolt. He was possibly the wealthiest Welshman of his day, with lands in North Wales and in Pembrokeshire. He had been trained in the law and in arms in England, but by the late 1390s was looking forward to a future of comfortable retirement in his charming fortified mansion of Sycherth, where he was accustomed to dispense a very civilised hospitality to his many friends. His rival and neighbour, Lord Grey of

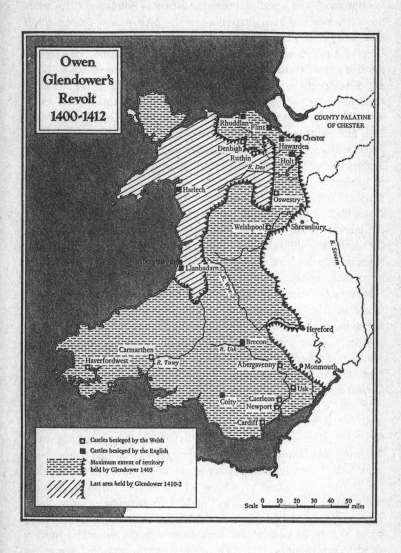

Owen Glendower's Revolt 1400-1412

COUNTY PALATINE OF CHESTER

Rhuddlan
Flint
Chester
Denbigh
Hawarden
Ruthin
Holt
R. Dee
Oswestry
Harlech
Welshpool
Shrewsbury
R. Severn
Aberystwyth
Llanbadarn
R. Wye
Hereford
Brecon
R. Usk
Carmarthen
Haverfordwest
R. Towy
Abergavenny
Monmouth
Tenby
Usk
Coity
Caerleon
Newport
Cardiff

◧ Castles besieged by the Welsh

■ Castles besieged by the English

Maximum extent of territory held by Glendower 1405

Last area held by Glendower 1410-2

Scale 0 10 20 30 40 50 miles

Ruthin, in his great Red Castle, was an ardent supporter of the Lancastrian cause and a personal friend of Henry of Bolingbroke. For years these two men had been quarrelling over a piece of land. Since Henry's accession the courts had given judgment in favour of the King's friend Grey, and Glendower had been insulted in London when he came to plead his case. From such petty beginnings arose the rebellion. Glendower's princely instincts were aroused and he led his men into Grey's lands which he proceeded to ransack. Once started this sort of action was difficult to stop and he moved into Shropshire burning and raiding. This first venture was soon quashed by the local English lords but Owen, with his lands now confiscated, found it very easy to exploit anti-English feeling and spread the revolt. His cousins, the Tudor brothers of Anglesey, soon joined him, and when he raised the ancient red dragon standard of Wales, men from all over North and, later, South Wales flocked to join him in revolt. Burning and pillaging the lands of the marcher lords and those Welshmen who refused to support him, Glendower was difficult to crush. His army of mountaineers with their bases in Snowdonia rarely risked a major engagement, but were masters of guerilla warfare.

Henry IV's reaction to the revolt was to sub-contract its suppression to the marcher lords under the nominal leadership of Prince Henry, whose headquarters were established at Chester. The Prince, still only thirteen, was too young to be the real leader, so he was supplied with a guardian and mentor, while the King contented himself with an annual expedition to punish the rebels. These expeditions were nearly always farcical and sometimes disastrous. Year after year the King turned up with a large army, and then together with his son's forces swept in an aimless fashion round North Wales. The Welshmen disappeared into their safe places in the mountains or raided the King's baggage-train. The rain poured down, particularly during the expedition of 1402, when 'night after night the soldiers lay in the open, drenched to the skin, and half-starved'. There were many who suspected the Welsh witches and magicians of thus washing King Henry's magnificent army away. Then wet, tired and herding a few miserable prisoners, the King went home, and the Welshmen came back down from the mountains to carry on with their raiding. By 1402 Owen was firmly in control. The marcher lords clung desperately to their castles, but the rest of the country was his. Now calling himself Prince of Wales, he sought by diplomacy to extend his revolt, and finally had success in the arrival of a French expeditionary force in Milford Bay in 1405. Before then he had already captured two of the great castles of the principality, Harlech and Aberystwyth. Perhaps even more important had been the capture of two extremely distinguished prisoners. In the winter of 1401–2 he had ridden over the wild hills dividing his property from Lord Grey's, and had managed to draw his great enemy out of his stronghold and seize him. The enormous price that Grey had to pay to get out of Owen's hands was to ruin him and provided much-needed finance for the rebellion. In the spring of 1402 Owen raided into Herefordshire, and after a savage battle captured Edmund Mortimer, the most powerful of all the marcher lords and the uncle of King Richard's true heir. Mortimer, no great friend of Henry IV, decided that alliance was preferable to imprisonment and ransom, married Glendower's daughter and ordered his tenants to join the revolt. Who was now the Prince of Wales?

Prince Henry's first guardian at Chester was the famous Hotspur, son of the Earl of Northumberland. A contemporary of the Prince's father, he was like Bolingbroke a renowned jouster and knight, the darling of the tournament crowds, whose popularity extended to a fashionable imitation of his stutter. Shakespeare, using pardonable licence, makes Hotspur Prince Hal's contemporary – 'this Hotspur Mars in swathing clothes, this infant warrior' – but he was in fact a very experienced man in his late thirties who probably made a strong impression on the Prince. Normally an impulsive man, whose military skill was often jeopardised by his impetuosity, he followed in Wales a careful and fairly conciliatory policy which had some success and might indeed have brought the revolt to an early end. However his guardianship of the Prince was brought to a sudden close in 1401, when, fed up with the King's failure to pay his troops, he threw up all his Welsh appointments, and went back to the more congenial occupations of border-raiding and killing Scotsmen, against whom he was to gain the most resounding victory of his career in the following year at the battle of Homildon Hill. Prince Henry was unlucky in his guardians, for the next one, Hugh le Despenser, a marcher lord, soon died. There is a charming letter extant in which the Prince writes to his father for a new governor and expresses his great regret at Hugh's death. By 1403 his governor was another Percy, Thomas Earl of Worcester, probably the best soldier of that soldierly family, but by this time the Prince, now sixteen, was being given more freedom in his military activity.

It would be tedious to give too many details of the Welsh revolt, which was an exceedingly confused affair with several different campaigns under different marcher lords going on at the same time. Suffice it to say that English policy was to hold their castles, match Glendower's raiding with raiding of their own, and to rely for a final ending of the revolt on exhaustion and the offer of very generous pardons. An example of what a raid involved is given by a letter written by Prince Henry in the summer of 1403. He set off from Shrewsbury and marched into the lands which belonged to Owen 'where we thought we should have found him, if he had an inclination to fight'. Owen was not there, so they caused the whole place to be burnt and then marched into Owen's other major property and burnt that too. Prisoners were taken and killed, ransom being too generous for captured Welshmen. The Prince then marched into Merionethshire and 'there we wasted a fair land and one well-inhabited'. But then, only a few weeks after setting out, he ran out of money to pay his troops. This was a perennial problem for all Henry IV's commanders. By no means ungenerous, he was just unable to raise enough cash for all his commitments. He had to pay off all his supporters, maintain his regal state, and put down numerous rebellions, and to do this he needed to extract money from Parliaments who made use of his weak title to the throne to refuse him taxes if he did not make concessions. For this reason the reign of Henry IV has been seen as one of extreme importance in the history of that control of the monarch by Parliament, which is one of the most precious gems in the Whig interpretation of history. But Parliament's gains were largely illusory, and Henry was able to throw off its tutelage once he had gained control of his kingdom. Lack of cash was a very real problem for his son, fighting for the Crown in Wales, and fills his correspondence. 'For the rebels hear each day whether we shall be paid, and they know well that without payment we cannot abide.' Prince Henry had to sell his jewels and pawn his plate to combat Glendower's rebellion, and though, unlike Hotspur, he stuck to the job, he knew that sooner or later his men would leave him if they received no pay. There was little booty to be won in Wales.

As it turned out, it was rather fortunate for the Lancastrian cause that Prince Henry did not have enough money to prolong his Welsh campaign in the summer of 1403. For while he was writing begging letters to his father stirring events were happening. On the same day that the King wrote a letter announcing his intention of joining his loyal subjects, the Percies, in a raid on Scotland, Henry Hotspur raised

4 John of Gaunt, Henry v's grandfather, being granted Aquitaine by Richard ii.
Miniature from the chronicle of Enguerrand de Monstrelet

2 (*above*) The Great Hall of John of Gaunt's castle at Kenilworth. John of Gaunt built a whole series of state apartments in the Angevin castle to make it more comfortable for his household

3 (*below left*) Dancing, from an early fifteenth-century manuscript (Bodleian Ms Douce 364 f.8)

4 (*below right*) Knights at dinner in a Great Hall, from a fifteenth-century Flemish manuscript (Bodleian Ms Douce 383 f.2v)

Henry v loved music – both listening and playing. At the age of ten he owned a harp which he could probably play. 5 (*left*) Fifteenth-century oak corbels from a Suffolk church showing angels holding a harp and a viol, a six-stringed instrument. 6 (*right*) An angel playing a rebeck, an early form of fiddle with three strings. From an early fifteenth-century piece of English stained glass

7 (*left*) Thomas of Woodstock, Duke of Gloucester, was Richard's youngest uncle and one of the Lords Appellant. In 1397 he was arrested on suspicion of plotting against the King. He was imprisoned in Calais and strangled before he could be brought to trial

8 (*below*) In 1398 Richard II took his revenge on the last two of the Lords Appellant, Henry Bolingbroke, Earl of Derby, and Thomas Mowbray, Duke of Norfolk. They had quarrelled and it was decided to resolve their quarrel by trial by combat, but at the last minute Richard stopped the battle. Instead, he exiled the contestants: Bolingbroke for ten years and Mowbray for life. In this manuscript illustration, Richard is shown banishing the two men

9 One panel of the Wilton Diptych showing Richard II being presented to the Virgin Mary (not shown) by his patron saints: King Edmund – the English king who was martyred by the Vikings–Edward the Confessor and St John the Baptist. Richard wears around his neck his personal symbol, the white hart

10 (*above left*) In the summer of 1399, Richard set off for Ireland, with most of his retinue, to quell a rebellion. This miniature portrays the King in full armour leaving London. Above him flies the quartered arms of England and France

11 (*above right*) While Richard was in Ireland, Bolingbroke sailed from Boulogne to Ravenspur to claim his Lancastrian inheritance. As he marched across England, he found that support for the King had faded away and at his entrance into London he was acclaimed by the chief citizens

12 (*below*) Bolingbroke at Chester Castle with the Dukes of Surrey and Exeter. (Bolingbroke is the figure in black, Surrey and Exeter are kneeling before him.) These two Dukes were members of the Holland family – Richard's mother, Joan, 'the Fair Maid of Kent', had made a previous marriage to Sir Thomas Holland. Both were friends of Richard, and therefore dangerous to Bolingbroke

13 (*left*) Owen Glendower in battle, a silverpoint drawing from the *Life of Richard Beauchamp, Earl of Warwick*

14 (*below*) Harlech Castle in Merionethshire. By the time of Glendower's revolt, Harlech and Aberystwyth had become two great royalist strongholds of the principality. Glendower captured Harlech in 1404 and Henry could not regain it until 1409: its fall marked the end of the Welsh revolt

15 (*above*) The coronation of Henry IV, which took place in Westminster Abbey on 13 October 1399. Henry of Monmouth, now Prince of Wales, carried the sword of justice at the ceremony

16 (*below*) Archbishop Arundel preaching the cause of Henry IV. Thomas Arundel had been banished by Richard for his part in the activities of the Lords Appellant, but was reinstated by Henry

17 (*left*) Henry Percy, Earl of Northumberland (to the left of the group), bringing a message to Richard from Bolingbroke. Northumberland was a great warrior, and had done a great deal to bring about Bolingbroke's success in his bid for the throne. By 1403, he, his son Hotspur, and his brother Thomas, Earl of Worcester, had quarrelled badly with Henry IV and were in open revolt

18 (*below*) A letter from Henry Hotspur to the King's Council

19 The battle of Shrewsbury, which took place in July 1403, between Henry's army and the forces of the Percies. They were about equal in strength and the pitched battle that ensued was to be Prince Henry's savage education in the art of warfare. One of the great features of the battle was the Cheshire archers, wearing the Ricardian badge and fighting for the Percies

20 Effigy of Henry IV from his tomb in Canterbury Cathedral

Hunting was one of the principal pursuits of courtiers during the fifteenth century. Henry's cousin, Edward of York, was an expert on the subject and has given us a treatise on hunting in England

21 (*above*) Detail from the fifteenth-century Hardwick Hunting Tapestry, showing a boar-hunt. 22 (*below*) A hunting party watching a stag swimming a stream, from a French manuscript of the second half of the fifteenth century (Bodleian Ms Douce 336 f.58)

23 Falconry, a panel from the Hardwick Hunting Tapestry

24 Thomas, Duke of Clarence, Henry IV's second son, from his effigy in Canterbury Cathedral. Thomas was impetuous and anxious to achieve glory to match up to his elder brother. It was these qualities which cost him his life at Baugé in 1421

25 (*left*) Humphrey, Duke of Gloucester, Henry IV's fourth and youngest son. Humphrey played a relatively small role in government during his brother's reign, but came to the fore during the minority of his nephew, Henry VI

26 (*below*) Duke Humphrey's Library in the Bodleian, viewed from the Selden End. In 1439, Humphrey, Duke of Gloucester, gave the first of a series of generous gifts of books to Oxford University to create a library. Five years later, the University decided to build a library over the Divinity School, and to offer Humphrey the title of Founder

27 Henry v being crowned, from his chantry chapel in Westminster Abbey

the standard of revolt at Chester. This revolt of the Percies was the most dangerous challenge to the Lancastrians before the rise of the House of York. Although they justified themselves by many grievances, there is no doubt that the true reason for their revolt was jealousy at the success of the House of Lancaster. Kingmakers faced by an over-mighty King, they decided to change their allegiance, possibly to the young Earl of March or an imaginary Richard, more likely to King Hotspur, founder of a Percy dynasty. That they failed was due to poor planning, a certain amount of bad luck and the military competence of Henry IV.

Hotspur had set out from the north with 'eight score horse', who included some very distinguished Scottish prisoners whom he had captured the year before at the battle of Homildon. These had been promised to be released from their ransom and well rewarded 'if it chanced the said King Henry to be vanquished and put from the crowne', and included the Earl of Douglas, leader of the traditional enemies of the Percies whose rivalry forms the theme of the Ballad of Chevy Chase. Hotspur's aim was to raise the men of Cheshire and the northern Welsh marches, where Ricardian sympathy was still strong, and then in conjunction with his uncle, Thomas Percy, Earl of Wor-cester, to seize the Prince of Wales at Shrewsbury. Once holding the King's son as hostage and secure in the fortifications of Shrewsbury, he could afford to wait for the rest of his allies, his father, who was raising another army in the north, and the Welsh hordes of Glendower and Mortimer, before attacking the King. There seems no doubt that if all these forces had combined they would have destroyed the Lancastrian cause for ever.

The plan was foiled by the extreme speed with which Henry IV moved once he heard details of the revolt. Egged on by his very com-petent and energetic ally, the renegade Scotsman, George Dunbar, he drove his men across the Midlands towards Shrewsbury, raising more troops as he went. The race was extremely close, some chroniclers stating that the King only reached his son's headquarters a few hours before Hotspur. The latter withdrew to a strong position to the north of the town, where, with his right flank resting on the Severn and his rear protected by rising ground, he encamped for the night. On the next morning, 21 July 1403, the Percies sent their defiant challenge to the King. 'We do intend to prove with our hands personally against thee Henry Duke of Lancaster unjustly presuming and named King of

England, without title of right, but only of thy guile.' Henry attempted to conciliate and persuade the Percies of their folly, but events had now moved too far and neither side trusted the other sufficiently for there to be any other outcome but battle.

Despite the military background to the period, pitched battles were extremely rare in late medieval warfare. Prince Henry was to fight in only two in his life, this savage internecine struggle at Shrewsbury and the more glamorous affair at Agincourt. The battle of Shrewsbury, if exciting, must have been an extremely unpleasant experience. The sixteen-year-old Prince of Wales commanding the royal left had to lead his men up sloping ground against an army commanded by two of his former governors, for one of whom he clearly felt great affection. As he struggled up the slope he was to experience the full effects of what had been the secret of English military success for the last sixty years – a barrage of arrows fired downhill by the superb Cheshire and Welsh archers, many of them wearing once again their Ricardian white hart badges. But the courage and leadership which were to take English arms so far in the future were already present in the young Prince. Although wounded in the face by a rebel arrow, he disregarded the advice of his entourage to retire and fought the long day out.

From midday to nightfall the evenly matched armies raged. The hardest fighting was naturally around the person of the King for, despite the large numbers involved, the battle was something of a personal encounter between two of the most famous knights of the day, Hotspur and Bolingbroke. The desperate Hotspur with a band of knights struck time and again to cleave a passage through to the royal standard. But the crafty Bolingbroke, anticipating the concentration of the battle on his own person, had taken the unchivalrous precaution of dressing some of his household knights in the royal surcoat to confuse the issue. It was an effective ruse, and Hotspur may have killed two or three kings before he in his turn was felled by an unknown hand as he raised his vizor to wipe his brow after his exertions. The death of Hotspur decided the issue, though the battle was extremely close, and 'so scattered was the field that when night fell, and the two armies separated, neither knew which had the victory, and they lay down in mixed heaps, weary and beaten and bleeding'. But in fact the defeat of the rebels was total. Thomas Percy was captured and executed, his head being placed on London Bridge. Hotspur, who had first been buried at Whitchurch by one of his great rivals Thomas Neville, Lord

Furnival, was disinterred, his body displayed to the world to convince those partisans doubtful of the death of so redoubtable a warrior, and his head set on the gate of York. His father, the Earl of Northumberland, prevented by illness and the speed of the King's march from being present at the battle, made his peace with Henry, who once again showed a surprising and rather unwise gift for mercy. After he had made his submission, the old Earl rode out of York at the King's side, under the festering head of his son.

The Prince's conduct in the battle and his increasing years persuaded his father to give him more and more control of the suppression of the Welsh rebellion. Glendower's strength was hardly affected at all by the defeat of the Percies. The story that he watched the battle from an oak tree on the banks of the Severn to see which side would win is almost certainly apocryphal. He was probably fighting in Pembrokeshire at the time, but what is certain is that the following year, 1404, was the zenith of his power. From then on his fortunes began to ebb. Early in 1405 the marcher Lord Talbot won an important victory against superior forces at Grosmont, and in March the Prince himself won an engagement near Usk which was 'attended by great slaughter that was for severity scarcely ever exceeded in Wales'.

But it was hard to put the Welsh down. Shortly after these setbacks, Owen seemed to be again supreme. In the spring he signed the famous tripartite convention by which he, Sir Edmund Mortimer and the Earl of Northumberland were to divide up England and Wales amongst them. Owen was to have all Wales and a considerable part of the west of England; Northumberland the north of England and the north Midlands; and Mortimer the rest. In May the King was faced by another major rebellion, led once again by old Henry Percy of Northumberland, this time in conjunction with no less a person than Archbishop Scrope of York. In August a large French expeditionary force landed in Wales. How could Lancaster survive so many blows? But by the end of the year all was comparatively quiet. Henry, once again moving fast, quashed the Northern rebellion with the aid of the Nevilles, and then, tired now of useless conciliation, shocked the Christian world by executing the Archbishop. The French went home, disappointed by the poverty of the booty to be found in a Wales ravaged by five years of civil war. Northumberland was still at large, now in Scotland, now in Wales, but finally the old warrior was cornered and killed by the Sheriff of Yorkshire at Bramham Moor in 1408. The revolt of the Percies was over. Hotspur's son and his grandsons were all to die in civil wars — ironically in the Lancastrian cause in the Wars of the Roses.

Having survived the fateful year of 1405, the Lancastrians were able to pay more attention to the suppression of the Welsh revolt. The Prince was now in charge, and though the business was slow, he moved steadily towards the final pacification of Wales. He and his captains now understood well the realities of Welsh warfare. No longer did great armies flounder through the Welsh bogs in pointless campaigns only to be sent 'bootless home, and weather-beaten back'. Now the English relied on the relentless pressure of small bands to wear down the resistance of the rebels. And to these exhausted rebels they offered liberal terms of pardon if they gave up the now unequal struggle. The policy was very effective. In 1406, following the example of the South Welsh, two thousand men of Anglesey submitted. By 1407 Owen was confined to the mountainous centre and west of the country, but his position was by no means hopeless, as he was still in possession of the two great castles of Harlech and Aberystwyth.

Prince Henry had several years of successful siege warfare in front of him, but he did not shine particularly in the reduction of his own Welsh strongholds. Leaving Harlech to the Talbots, he laid siege to Aberystwyth in 1407, joined by large numbers of knights eager to be in at the end of the Welsh revolt. The siege was not quite the social success that they had expected. The King's guns brought round by sea were ineffective against the enormous walls of the Edwardian castle. Assault impossible, the Prince was forced to sit down to starve the garrison out. Following the convention of the day the garrison agreed to submit unless relieved by a certain date. Most of the besieging force, including Prince Henry, then went home, sure that there was no relief available and unwilling to sit out what turned out to be the coldest winter in living memory. It was a foolish mistake which the Prince did not repeat in his French campaigns. While the Prince was away, Glendower slipped into the castle and rallied the garrison, so that instead of returning for a triumphal delivery of the keys in the spring, the Prince had to start all over again, before the castle was finally surrendered in the late summer of 1408. Harlech lasted out till the following year and at last it might be said that the Welsh revolt was over.

Indeed it could be said that the troubles of the Lancastrian usurpation were over. In the North danger from Scotland had been allayed by the lucky capture of the heir to the Scottish throne on his way to

France. Soon to become king, as James I, he was held by the English for eighteen years, and the threat that he might be sent home to Scotland was normally sufficient to keep the Scottish regent, the Duke of Albany, in check. Further south, too, the dangers appeared to have disappeared. The Percies were all dead, Mortimer had died at the siege of Harlech, Glendower's family were nearly all dead or captured. But Glendower still lived. He was still fighting with a small band in 1412. And indeed there are some who say that he and his men continue to live and are asleep on their arms in a cave in the Vale of Gwent, waiting for another day to sally forth against the English.

3
A Problem of Generations
1408–13

When Prince Henry finally captured Aberystwyth Castle he was just twenty-one years old. Since he first rode at his father's side towards Scotland in 1400 he had done little else but fight to maintain Bolingbroke's usurpation of the throne. It was a rude education, but one not unsuitable for a medieval king. From the early days under Hotspur's tutelage till the day when he rode for ever out of his wet and mountainous principality, he had struggled to establish himself as a real Prince of Wales against the counter-claims of the ageing Welsh country gentleman who now lived a precarious life in the caves and forests of Snowdonia. In the process he must have learnt much about military life, though it would be wrong to say that he had displayed many signs of his later military genius. He had learned to lead and fight, he knew what it was like to be wounded, to march through the rain and besiege a castle. He knew how to make friends of his captains and he knew what it was like to fight against a former friend. All this was useful experience to have gained so young. For the next seven years he was to live on a different stage, a stage where talking rather than fighting settled the issues.

Even if we discount a little the hyperbole of chroniclers, the Prince seems to have been a good-looking member of a good-looking family. About average height, he had a long, handsome ruddy face with a straight nose and thick brown hair. Young and strong, a brave leader and a born showman, he was a great favourite in the capital where he settled down in a 'right fair and stately house' called Coldharbour in Eastcheap. Everyone praised the handsome young Prince. Parliament praised him for his obedience to his father, his courage and his willingness to listen to advice. Tradesmen praised him for his extravagance.

His friends praised him for his generosity and loyalty. And they had good cause. His surviving correspondence is studded with evidence of his eagerness to reward or help his friends: letters to bishops asking for jobs for his clerks or thanking them for favours to his servants; a letter to an abbot to whom he is sending his chancellor for treatment for his sciatica; a letter to a bishop to ask pardon for one of his servants, excommunicated for having carelessly allowed some of the Prince's hounds to kill animals as he was making his way through the bishop's park in Sussex. Indeed one of the most famous stories of the Prince's madcap days involves him striking the Chief Justice in the face as a result of some suspected injustice to one of his servants. He was a very popular prince.

All this was somewhat in contrast to his father. The handsome, brave Bolingbroke of fourteenth-century jousting fame was now a sick, tired man. In 1405 he contracted some unpleasant disease which temporarily affected his appearance and sometimes led to complete incapacity to rule. What it was no one knows. Contemporaries thought it was leprosy, God's punishment for the execution of an archbishop. Some modern historians think it was a venereal disease incurred in the European adventures of his youth. But medical historians, with a no doubt admirable contempt for kings, tend to diagnose all mysterious royal diseases as venereal. Suffice it that the King was ill, and in the winter of 1408 seemed ready to die, a fact which left control of the country in the hands of his eldest son. Prince Henry did not seem too happy at the recovery of his royal father in the following year, and the consequent curtailment of his temporary power.

As early as 1406 it had been rumoured that the Prince would like to depose his sickening father, and opposition to the King's authority had begun to develop in the King's own Council. By 1409 this opposition was clear. Two parties, both loyal to the Lancastrian cause, had formed – one around the King and one around the Prince. For the most part division followed age. The Prince's party was led by the King's two surviving half-brothers, the Beauforts. Henry Beaufort, the future Cardinal, at present Bishop of Winchester, and Sir Thomas, soon to be Earl of Dorset, later Duke of Exeter, made a good partnership, one an able diplomat and administrator, the other a competent soldier, both talented men. They were supported by two young fighting earls, close friends of the Prince and sons of two of the Lords Appellant on whom King Richard had had his revenge in 1397 – Warwick, 'the master of courtesy' who returned to England in 1410 after a triumphant jousting tour and pilgrimage abroad, and Arundel who had already seen service at the Prince's side in Wales. Also beginning to make a showing was the Prince's friend and future archbishop, William of Wykeham's protégé, the ex-shepherd boy, Henry Chichele, Bishop of St Davids. All these were to be the strongest supporters of the Prince both in England and in France when he became King. To this group should be added two of the Prince's young brothers, John and Humphrey. John of Lancaster, later Duke of Bedford, had had a similar youth to that of his elder brother, being given military command on the Scottish border and much of the Percies' lands after the failure of their revolt in 1403. Far and away the most trustworthy and competent of the Prince's brothers, he was to play an invaluable part in Henry's life by looking after England while he was seeking glory in France. Humphrey, later Duke of Gloucester, had had less to do and was already showing signs of the dissolute bibliophile and troublemaker he was to become in later years.

The King's party, headed by Archbishop Arundel, uncle of the Prince's friend, with whom he had quarrelled over their respective lands in Sussex, was smaller and older, and since it seemed bound to be the eventual loser was not quite so studded with illustrious names. It will suffice to mention the one young member, the King's other son, Thomas, who had become estranged from the Beauforts and his brother after a rather sordid quarrel about an inheritance. Thomas had married the widow of the eldest Beaufort, John, Earl of Somerset, and claimed 30,000 marks which Bishop Beaufort had received as his brother's executor. In the row which followed Prince Henry had upheld his uncle against his brother. Thomas, later Duke of Clarence, was in many ways the most attractive of all Henry IV's sons. Handsome, energetic and brave, a sportsman and a soldier, he spent most of his life attempting in dramatic and courageous ways to outshine his elder brother, to whom, once King, he was however always loyal.

These two parties made themselves effective through the control of the Council of which the Prince was head from 1410 to the October of the following year, when the King abruptly dismissed him and the Beauforts, and ruled with the help of Archbishop Arundel till the end of the reign. The main difference in the policies of the two parties was in their attitude towards France. However shaky their right to the English throne, both Prince Henry and his father were clear that as

Kings of England they had taken over the Plantagenet claim to the kingdom of France, so weakly defended by the late King Richard, who had made a twenty-five-year truce with France in 1396 and married the French King's daughter, Isabel, as his second wife. In the troubled early years of his reign Henry had not dared to annoy France more than necessary, and he had had much trouble in trying to persuade the French to take back Richard's young Queen, without having to pay back too much of her dowry. It had even been suggested that Prince Henry should marry the late King's widow, but to no avail. At last Richard's widow, still a child, 'departed from London to go to her father, clad in mourning weeds, and showing a countenance of lowering and evil aspect to King Henry, and scare opening her lips, as she went her way'. Since then relations with France had been none too good, and, truce or not, a French force had gone to aid Glendower in 1405. But now things were rather different. England was quiet while France was in a state of civil war, in which Burgundian slaughtered Armagnac and Armagnac slaughtered Burgundian, while both indiscriminately slaughtered, robbed and terrorised the townsfolk and the peasants. Surely, with a little skill, Burgundian could be played off against Armagnac, while both were robbed and pillaged by the indifferent English?

Civil war was not a particularly unusual state in France, or, for that matter, as we have seen, in England. The Crown of France quite often found that it had three or four separate civil wars on its hands at once. For, despite the successes of the Capetians in expanding the domain proper, that is the part of France ruled directly by the King, this was still only some two-thirds of the kingdom. Surrounding the domain proper were the four great fiefs – Flanders, Brittany, Burgundy and Gascony. The Valois kings of France, if they were strong, might be able to control these fiefs but, if they were weak or if the domain proper was itself contested between rival parties, then their great vassals had a strong incentive to push for a greater degree of autonomy and establish themselves as independent princes. This was exactly what had happened in the early fifteenth century.

Indeed the King of France was not just weak, he spent much of his time in increasingly long bouts of insanity. The story of the beginning of his madness is a sad and strangely moving one. In 1392 the pleasure-loving and already feeble Charles VI was riding at the head of his knights to punish his rebellious vassals in Brittany. The army was riding slowly across the plain to the west of Le Mans under a burning sun, when a lunatic emerged from the edge of the forest and was not checked until he had reached the King's horse. He seized the bridle and shouted at him in an almost incoherent gibber that he was betrayed. Shaken by the lunatic the King's mind broke. In the heat and the blinding light he thought that the accidental striking of a lance against a helmet was the signal for an attack on him. He threw himself upon his suite and attacked them. The now insane King was pulled off by his attendants, but such fits were to recur for the rest of his long reign.

It really was an unfortunate time for France to have a mad King, for it led inevitably to a struggle for power amongst his close relatives. These had all greatly increased their nuisance potential as a result of the very large territories given to his brothers by the late King Charles V. Loyal during the successful reign of Charles V, they and their descendants were to split France apart under his mad son. There is no need to go into great details of this squabble for power. Very soon the main protagonists had made themselves clear. On the one side stood Philip the Bold, Duke of Burgundy, the youngest son of Charles V, whose marriage to the richest heiress in Europe, Margaret of Flanders, had been arranged by his father in the teeth of opposition from Edward III of England, who had wanted her for his fourth son, later Duke of York. Edward had been foiled chiefly by the efforts of Urban V, one of the last of the French puppet popes at Avignon, who had declared the relationship to be within the limits prohibited by canon law. With his wife's lands and further grants from his father, Philip ruled a great principality from the mouth of the Somme to the mouth of the Scheldt, together with his own and his wife's lands in Burgundy. His policy of aggrandisement of the power of this Burgundian state was to be carried on by his son, John the Fearless.

The main opponent to Duke Philip was the Duke of Orléans, the mad King's libertine younger brother, who was supported by his remaining two uncles. The lands of these three opponents of Duke Philip were mainly in the south and west of France. The power struggle between the two parties with its background of hatred, murder, diplomacy and quite often open war was to continue for a generation, but it was given a new intensity in 1407 when the Duke of Orléans was assassinated on the orders of John the Fearless, who had succeeded his father as Duke of Burgundy in 1404. By 1410 the two parties were known as the Armagnacs, after Bernard of Armagnac, a veteran soldier whose daughter was married to the young son of the murdered Duke, and the Burgundians.

The main basis of diplomacy in the later years of Henry IV and in the reign of his son was to play these two parties off against each other. But the scope was greater than that. Of the two remaining fiefs, one was Gascony, which as the last remnant of the great Angevin Empire was the heritage of the King of England. But the other, Brittany, was disputed between two rival parties as was France itself. There was always scope for English diplomacy to exploit this dispute, at worst to make a truce with Brittany, at best to bring in Breton captains on the English side. Outside the realm of France there was still more scope for diplomacy. A ring of states, large and small, was often only too eager to exploit the weakness of France. Their neutrality or armed friendship might be expensive, as Edward III had found, but their alliance was worth exploring.

In this confused scene the problem was which side to choose. Almost as if it was necessary to be opposed on this score, since there was little else to be opposed about, Henry IV favoured the Armagnacs, while the Prince of Wales favoured the Burgundians. Meanwhile both the French parties, seeking help to overcome each other, wooed the English. English demands varied according to the situation in France. At the very least they always demanded assistance in maintaining their possessions in France, particularly the great wool staple port of Calais, commanding the narrows, and the wine port of Bordeaux. As the civil wars intensified and each side needed the English more, the English demands grew. Such demands could be legion: the daughter of the Duke of Burgundy with a large dowry as a wife for the Prince of Wales; the daughter of the King of France, Katherine, with an even greater dowry; the balance of the ransom of King John, captured at Poitiers in 1356; the whole of Aquitaine; the whole of the Angevin Empire; the whole of the Angevin Empire plus the duchy of Normandy. By the early years of Henry V's reign the English were demanding all these things in addition to the Crown of France itself. They all made useful counters in the diplomatic game. In 1411, however, the Prince's Council had rather more modest ambitions. As soon as the Prince was in power he set about putting the royal finances in order, a very necessary task, but one which clearly had war-like thinking behind it, since he was already drawing up estimates for the cost of Calais in time of war. Meanwhile negotiations with Burgundy ending in vague promises by both sides were sufficient to tempt the Prince and Beaufort to find out if English arms were rusty. An English expeditionary force under the Earl of Arundel was sent to assist the Duke of Burgundy. They had some easy successes and provided useful indications of the likely result of future expeditions. Nothing much came of this, however, for as we have seen, the King was back in control by November. Somewhat to the embarrassment of all, he reversed Prince Henry's policy and sent another expedition under his son, Thomas, now Duke of Clarence, to aid the Armagnacs in the following year. Clarence's expedition made a handsome profit. After he had made a profitable *chevauchée* into Anjou and the Orléanais, the two French parties made a truce and pooled their resources to pay him to go back home again. The payment of warrior bands to go somewhere else was a rather necessary feature of late medieval conditions.

It was during this interval between the end of the Welsh rebellion and his accession to the throne, that the Prince of Wales acquired his reputation as a madcap. Although there is no historical justification for Shakespeare's rascally companions to the young Prince Hal, it seems quite clear that there was some truth in the reputation. And indeed it would be rather strange if there were not. For a boy who had lived in military camps since the age of thirteen to have totally avoided the normal amusements of military men would have been strange. For the Prince to lead his followers in riotous pranks was not strange either. He was after all a leader. And if Wales or Chester offered scanty fare for licentious soldiery, London could always be visited during the winter months when medieval warfare normally drew to a halt. Once the rebellion was over, Henry made London his main home and no doubt continued to enjoy himself when not engaged in his Council duties. But we know in fact very little about such enjoyments. He left no bastards from a riotous youth as did his episcopal uncle, Bishop Beaufort. The sort of details left to us are one or two stories involving fights in the streets and similar affrays, and much-quoted passages from the chroniclers in which it is stated that the Prince 'fervently followed the service of Venus as well as Mars' or 'exercised meanly the feats of Venus and of Mars so long as his father lived'. Too many writers mention this sort of thing to leave much doubt that he was an unusually wild young man, 'a rollicker who would swear, drink, dance and revel the night'. For details readers will have to join Shakespeare in using their imagination.

The combination of reports of his son's pranks, his popularity, and suspicions of his disloyalty, must have been upsetting for his father, who had no doubt forgotten his youth, as so many fathers do. On at least two occasions matters between them seem to have got really serious, until the Prince, with an astonishing combination of arrogance and humility, made peace with his father. Arrogance in the city with his retinue of armed men amidst the cheers of the crowds; humility in his father's presence as he pledged his loyalty and made his obeisance. But the days of Henry of Bolingbroke were drawing to a close; after a last seizure he died in March 1413 in the Jerusalem Chamber of Westminster Palace. Whether the Prince tried on the crown as his father lay dying is another of those unconfirmed stories which surround the youth of the future hero. One eulogist of the Prince accepts the story and justifies his hero's premature action by explaining that, if the Prince had not taken it, someone else might well have done so, maybe to present it to the Earl of March, now at the age of twenty-two a rather more suitable candidate for king than in 1399. Such worries no doubt filled the mind of the dying King as he struggled between the dictates of his conscience and his hopes for the future of his House. A French chronicler makes the King ask the Prince how he shall have any right to the crown 'since as you know well I never had any'. The Prince's answer is clear and convincing. 'My lord, as you have kept and guarded it by the sword, so do I intend to guard it all my life.'

4
A Christian Prince Prepares for War 1413–15

If the heavens had been quiet at Henry's birth, they were suitably impressive at his coronation. A terrible blizzard covered the land burying men, beasts and houses deep in snow. Sages searched the scriptures to interpret this omen of the new reign. The results were confusing. The whiteness of the snow proclaimed the new King's purity, its softness his mercy, but its coldness was the coldness of a stern and implacable justice, and the fury of the wind that spread the snow over the land was the fury of a King at war. All the sages were right, for Henry was all these things. Such ambiguity was a characteristic of his times. A man could not be at the same time a Christian knight and a successful knightly King in time of war without having a personality which is difficult for modern writers to interpret.

From the moment of his father's death Henry appears as a new man. No longer did he follow the service of Venus as well as Mars: no more swearing, drinking, dancing and revelling; no women from his accession till his marriage, and then only his wife. The life of a Christian King must be above reproach. There is not a suspicion of scandal about the behaviour of the new King. Pilgrimages, fasts, endowment of religious houses, thanksgivings for God's grace punctuate the story of his progress to glory. Following his progress was his private chapel, ensuring that the King heard his three masses a day and was scrupulous in his other religious activities. He was a very pious King.

He was loyal and merciful too; loyal to his friends and merciful to his father's enemies. Those friends who had helped him sow his wild oats in his youth, their services no longer required, were paid off generously. Those who had counselled and advised him and supported his opposition to his father now found themselves in control of the country. His uncles, the Beauforts, his friends the Earls of Warwick and Arundel, his younger brothers John and Humphrey, all the members of his Council as Prince of Wales, these were his main councillors as King. To his father's enemies he offered a general amnesty. In particular he singled out those young noblemen whose fathers had been King Richard's courtiers. The young Earls of Salisbury, Huntingdon and Oxford were now all in favour, their lands restored, and were to repay mercy with good service. Henry felt secure – secure enough to free the Earl of March, the true heir to the throne, from his long confinement; secure enough, by December of the first year of his reign, to remove the remains of King Richard from their inglorious resting place to the tomb that the late King had built for himself in Westminster Abbey. It was a sign that Henry was no usurper, but as the son of a usurper he could expiate his father's sins. It was also a sign that King Richard was really dead.

All indeed seemed quiet. The lords had rushed to take the oath of allegiance even before the coronation. The coronation had been a great success. The ceremony itself had been followed by a great feast in Westminster Hall. The tables were laden with magnificent dishes and were decorated with sugar and paste antelopes and eagles, from whose mouths illuminated texts hung out exhorting the new King to 'keep the law and guard the *foi*' and 'to have pity on the commonalty'. The King himself was moody, weighed down by his new responsibilities, and did not eat. But his guests, served by servants on horseback, enjoyed themselves and when the King's champion rode in to cry his challenge there was no reply.

All the lords seemed pleased with their new King. The common people, too, were happy. There was peace and plenty in the land; it was to be many years before the barons went to war again in a determined attempt to unseat the Lancastrian kings. In the meantime the peasants reaped the benefits of the horrors of the previous century. The succession of plagues and famines, of which the most dramatic manifestation was the Black Death of 1347–8, had taken the pressure off the land. As the pressure of overpopulation decreased, and as cultivation became concentrated on the better lands, so the amount of food per head increased. The price of corn fell and poor men were able to improve their standards of living, eating wheat instead of rye, and meat instead of wheat. Shortage of labour pushed up the general level of wages. Shortage of labour also forced the lords to abandon the old methods of cultivation in which they had farmed their own lands using serf or low-wage labour. Now, more and more, they rented out their lands to the prosperous and well-fed peasants, abandoning their attempts to enforce reactionary legislation aimed to keep wages down and the peasants tied to the soil. There was to be no peasants' revolt in Henry's reign.

Not everybody was happy, however. While Henry was presiding at the ceremony of the reburial of King Richard there was a strange restlessness in the countryside. A few weeks later, a chronicler could record movement along the roads which seemed to have something of the breathlessness of the White Rabbit about it. 'You might see the crowds drawn along by large promises from almost every country in the realm, hastening along by footpaths, high roads and byways to meet at the day and the hour at hand. When asked why they hurried thus and ran themselves nearly out of breath, they answered that they were going as fast as they could to join their Lord Cobham.'

Lord Cobham, formerly Sir John Oldcastle, was the leader of the Lollards. These seekers after an older and purer form of Christianity drew their inspiration from reading the new English Bible. Their intellectual strength came from Oxford, but for popular support they relied mainly on the new industrial groups, particularly the cloth-workers in the rapidly growing new centres of the countryside and the workers in those trades where literacy was usual or necessary. They believed that confession was not necessary for salvation and that bread remained bread after consecration. Above all they wished to destroy the power of the priests, especially that greatest priest of all, the Pope. One Pope was bad enough, but three was much worse: three Anti-Christs to pervert the sacred words of the Gospels. Henry's attitudes to such heretics was quite correct, and was shared by the majority of clerics and laymen of his day. The Church might not be perfect, and Henry was in the forefront of attempts to reform it, but heresy must be wiped out. Every possible effort should be made to allow Lollards to see the error of their ways, but if they insisted in their infamous beliefs, then only the fire could cleanse them. An event of 1409 illustrates well this attitude. A tailor had been condemned to the stake for heresy, and was being burned in the presence of Prince Henry. As the flames reached him he called out for mercy. The Prince ordered the fire to be extinguished, and called on the tailor to recant. The tailor refused, the fire was relit and the Prince watched him as he burned to death. Henry's orthodoxy was put to an even sterner test by the heresy of Oldcastle, for Oldcastle was a personal friend of his. He was a distinguished soldier who had been active in the suppression of the Welsh rebellion. But ideas which might have seemed merely unusual in Wales were frankly heretical in London. Soon Oldcastle had attracted the attention of the Church by his heretical opinions. Nothing that the King or the leading churchmen could do would make him repent of his errors, and when he was eventually brought to trial by Archbishop Arundel, with Henry's consent, he made little effort to defend himself. There was no alternative but to send the King's friend to the stake.

While Oldcastle was imprisoned in the Tower awaiting his sentence, he managed to escape and immediately set about planning a rebellion which would free the country from the bonds of orthodoxy. Details of the plot bear a marked resemblance to the plot of 1400, which had led to the desperate flight of Henry IV and his sons from the Twelfth Night celebrations at Windsor Castle. A picked band of conspirators, disguised as mummers, was to present itself before the court at Eltham and there capture the whole of the royal family. Meanwhile hundreds of small bands of Lollards were to make their way to the fields outside Temple Bar. A general rendezvous had been planned for the night of 9 January 1414. But the rebellion was a pathetic failure. Betrayed by the King's spies, the main conspirators were arrested, tortured and confessed. Meanwhile the unsuspecting bands continued to make their way to London where royal troops were awaiting them. Many managed to flee to safety, but many others, including most of the leaders, were hanged in batches of four at St Giles Fields before Henry declared a general amnesty. Oldcastle himself remained uncaptured and Henry was spared the sight of his former friend roasting to death. This pleasure was reserved for his brother Bedford, while the King himself was in France. The massacre of the conspirators left the Lollard movement leaderless. There were no more Lollard knights, and no religious change of any real moment could occur unless it was supported by some at least of the knights and barons. But Lollardy itself did not die.

With the lords quiet and the Lollards suppressed, it was time for King Henry to decide what to do with his inheritance. There can never have been much doubt in his mind. He would go to war to claim those parts of his inheritance so unjustly held by his royal cousin across the Channel. After so long a peace any other policy was unthinkable. War meant glory, excitement and adventure; above all war meant plunder.

And this was a just war; both the Church and Parliament supported it. As for the nobility, war against France was their way of life, a way of life of which they had been deprived for a generation. Their education, their talents, their whole code of behaviour was directed towards war. Indeed to be a noble was to be a warrior, it was the justification of their power. Of the seventeen members of the higher nobility alive when Henry set sail for France in 1415, only three did not fight in person during the King's reign – two were boys, and the third was blind. The rest formed the military leadership in France or on the Scottish border. It is hardly surprising that they supported war.

But in an increasingly legalistic age naked aggression needed to be dressed up in more peaceful garb. Before war must come diplomacy. The failure of diplomacy would provide a justification for war, and while diplomacy continued, war could be prepared. Between 1413 and 1415 the situation in France was particularly favourable to Henry. In the summer of 1413 his former ally the Duke of Burgundy, a favourite of the Parisian mob, had stood by while his pensioner, the butcher Caboche, had led a revolt of butchers, tripe-dealers, skinners and tanners against the Armagnacs. The revolt had got completely out of hand, and reaction against the butchery of the butchers had given the city to the Armagnacs. King Charles, in one of his periods of sanity, avowed himself an Armagnac, declared Burgundy a traitor and barred him from Paris. In April 1414 Charles left Paris with the Queen, the Dauphin and a great army under the leadership of the Dukes of Orléans, Bourbon and Bar to crush the Duke of Burgundy. Burgundy's pleas for pardon were ignored and the royal army, after sacking Soissons, sat down to besiege his great city of Arras. Although the siege was ultimately unsuccessful and the royal army crawled home to Paris ravaged by dysentery, the royal aggression had Burgundy looking frantically for allies. On another front the Armagnacs had also had some successes, and had abandoned the temporary alliance made with Henry iv in the last year of his reign. In November 1413 the Duke of Bourbon had marched into English Aquitaine and defeated an Anglo-Gascon force at Soubise. The Duke had then returned to Paris 'where he was fêted amidst general rejoicing and his gallant deeds and elegant dress were the talk of the great Parisian ladies'.

Exploiting the general scene of Armagnac ascendancy Henry and his envoys had little difficulty in coming to agreement with the Duke of Burgundy. By the end of 1413 Henry had agreed to be associated in war with the Burgundians against the Armagnacs, while the Duke had promised to remain neutral if Henry pressed his claim to the Crown of France, and to do homage to him if he won it. Secure on this side Henry turned his attention to the Armagnacs, able after Bourbon's raid to pose as the innocent victim of aggression. Here he played the old game of making such outrageous demands that they could never be accepted – the Crown of France, the whole of the former Angevin Empire, the duchy of Normandy, half of Provence, the unpaid ransom of King John, the hand of the French King's daughter and a dowry of two million French crowns. The Armagnac negotiators were extraordinarily conciliatory, but the gap between Henry's demands and possible concessions remained. It had to, for the whole point of the diplomacy was to make the future war just. If the King of France was not prepared to give up his Crown, several of his richest provinces and his daughter, then Henry really had no option but to carry on with his preparations for invasion to take by force what was his by right.

These preparations were well advanced by the time of the final breakdown of negotiations in early 1415. Preparations for invasion on the scale that Henry had in mind required an enormous amount of activity throughout the kingdom. Above all, invasion required the collection of large quantities of money, men and materials. In all these three fields the English had great advantages over the French. Money, in particular, which Henry as Prince of Wales had found so difficult to obtain, was supplied with comparative ease for his French campaigns. Indeed the historian Stubbs remarked that Henry's success 'in obtaining money, men and ships was little less than miraculous' compared with his father's reign. Both Parliament and the Church were very generous in agreeing to extra taxation on trade and estates, and most of his requirements were met through such extra taxation and from his own income as King and Duke of Lancaster. He could not meet all his requirements, however, and it was necessary to resort to borrowing on pledge of jewels and other assets, and by means of more or less forced loans, often on the pledge of future income. One of the greatest creditors of the Crown was Henry's uncle Bishop Beaufort. Despite the increases in taxation occasioned by Henry's wars they should not be considered in the light of the level of taxation required for modern warfare. At its height annual taxation per head was only equivalent to the wages of a carpenter for a few days. And what is more, the burden decreased as time went on. Not only did war pay for itself to a certain extent by the receipt of the gains of war in the form of the King's share of ransoms and prize-money, but also Henry was able to do what none of his predecessors had done successfully, to push the cost of the war on to the population of his conquered territories. As the English contribution declined, the contribution of the French, and especially the Normans, increased. The sources of royal income in Normandy included the taxation normally paid to the King of France, the income from the lands owned by the French King in Normandy, plus the income from the lands of lay and clerical lords who did not submit to Henry, and the normal gains of war, such as impositions on towns which resisted, ransoms and prize-money. By 1419–20 the King was receiving from his new territories nearly one-fifth of the revenue he received from the whole of England during the same period. Naturally enough this kind of administrative efficiency made his war extremely popular in England.

Men, too, were not hard to find. Though shortage of men might well be one of the main causes of the ultimate failure of the Lancastrian kings' policy in France, it does not seem to have been a very serious problem for Henry. Research has shown that the exaggerated numbers of soldiers mentioned by the chroniclers have no basis in fact, and that the armies of Henry v rarely exceeded ten thousand fighting men, that is to say well under one per cent of the population. To find ten thousand men to serve under a popular, and later conspicuously successful, commander in a country whose whole social structure was organised on military lines was really no problem. A successful leader meant booty and the possibility at least of pay. It also meant adventure and a fairly good chance of survival. A poor leader and a badly-run war almost certainly meant no pay, no booty and a high possibility of capture and exorbitant ransom demands or death. If numbers could not be made up with respectable men there were alternative sources of supply – for an outlaw, service in war might mean the possibility of a return to respectability. In some of the English armies of the fourteenth century as many as five per cent of the total numbers were murderers seeking a pardon. These very simple equations explain why the English had no trouble finding men willing to serve in the campaigns of Henry v, even though, contrary to nearly all precedent, this might mean spending several years abroad. There were to be compensations for this long exile, just as there were for participants in the successes of the early Crusades. For it was Henry's policy to grant property to his followers out of the lands of those Normans who refused to submit to him. The funds of many impoverished noble houses, such as those of two of his leading lieutenants, Thomas Montacute, Earl of Salisbury and Richard Beauchamp, Earl of Warwick, were replenished in Henry's wars, while lesser men, such as Sir John Fastolf, one of Henry's most successful knights, could create a fortune to lift them out of obscurity, even if they were unable to push themselves above their social superiors.

The actual techniques of raising an army for a foreign expedition had been evolved during the reign of Edward III, though Henry and his brother, Bedford, were to improve the efficiency of their administration. Once a war had been decided on, or even before, the leading lords and knights were ordered to state the number of troops they could bring to serve the King. These lords and captains, of whom some eighty served on Henry's 1417 campaign, would all be well-known to a military king and were all expected to be fit and ready for war at any time. Many of them served in fact as a sort of permanent reserve, financed by grants of land or annuities which had been given them in return for a promise to serve when summoned, and the soldiers who they promised to bring on campaign were often their own retainers or tenants. Their absence from the land would make little difference to the economy, for as the historian, MacFarlane, has pointed out, most of the actual combatants were 'gentlemen by birth and their servants . . . who had no other gainful employment than war and the collection of rent'. About three-quarters of the whole English army were the archers, now, after almost a century of continuous success in foreign wars, nearly professional soldiers, who enlisted for sheer love of fighting, desire for adventures and hope of plunder. The captains, then, would have little difficulty in finding the men to serve under them, and in fact their reply to the King's summons might take on a fairly stereotyped form, their company being the same as on the last campaign.

When the captains had stated the number of men they would bring, the next stage was for them to come to make contracts for service with the King. In these contracts, known as indentures, the captain promised to provide a stipulated number of men-at-arms and archers, normally in the ratio of one man-at-arms to three archers, together with their horses, equipment and arms for a certain period of time. They also promised to make a muster of their retinue from time to time before such officials as the King might appoint. In return for these promises the King promised to pay the captains, and as some earnest of his ability to do that, it was normal to pay the captains a quarter's wages in advance when they made their indentures. If the King had not enough money to pay the captains he again resorted to handing out pledges of jewellery. Indeed most of the Crown jewels must have been distributed amongst his captains and his creditors. Many of these were not redeemed until late in the following reign. Edward, Duke of York, received a golden alms dish, called the Tiger, made like a ship and standing on a bear, which was garnished with rubies and pearls. Thomas Montacute, Earl of Salisbury, bore away a large ship of silver over gilt, with twelve men-at-arms fighting on the deck, and at each end a castle. Whether bearing cash or jewels, the captains then went home and made separate contracts on the same lines with their own men. The King's brother, Thomas, Duke of Clarence, who contracted to bring the largest contingent of all, well over a thousand men, had to break up his pledge, the Crown Henry, to satisfy his followers. Some of the rubies, emeralds, pearls and sapphires from this crown were not redeemed until the early 1430s.

The next stage after the indenture was the muster. The efficiency of this institution under Henry v and Bedford was one of the most striking contrasts between the administration of the English and French armies. The object of the muster was twofold: first, to get the army together at a particular place, for example at the port of embarkation; secondly, and more important of the two when the army was in the field, to make sure that the captains were in fact carrying out their part of their bargain with the King. For, since the money paid to captains depended on the number and type of soldiers whom they had contracted to supply by their indentures, and whose names were all inscribed on the muster rolls, they had every incentive to cheat the Exchequer by pretending that their companies were up to full strength when they were not. If a captain had, for instance, contracted to supply a company of mounted archers which would consist of 'six archers, all on horseback, and well chosen men and likely persons, well and sufficiently armed, horsed, and arrayed, every man after his degree; that is to say . . . harness complete, with bassinet or salade with vizor, spear, axe, sword, and dagger; and all the said archers specially to have good jacks of defence, salades, swords, and sheeves of 40 arrows at least', then the mustering officer would make sure that all these things were present and correct. A man with no horse, or with his face unprotected by a vizor, was that much less use to his King, and therefore the contract was that much unfulfilled, and hence the wages would be cut. Like all bureaucrats, mustering officers sometimes overdid their zeal, particularly in later years in Normandy, but their general efficiency, especially when compared with contemporary French military administration, deserves much admiration. The institution of the muster and the noble attempt to pay the soldiers in advance prevented Henry's army from acquiring some of the attitudes of contemporary Frenchmen, who from non-payment of wages were forced to live entirely by pillage and blackmail. A letter from a French *routier* captain makes the point very clear, when he informs the Marshal of Burgundy that a truce is unthinkable unless he provides for him and his company some means of subsistence, 'for without wages we cannot sustain ourselves unless we make war'. An even more cynical view is reflected in a contemporary comment that a military disaster could well be an administrative triumph, since dead men need no pay.

The indentured English companies were not the only troops available to the King. He had his own household troops whose central element was the élite body of the knights of the household, the King's knights. He could also draw upon his subjects abroad. Especially important were the Gascons, who provided companies similar to those of the English captains, and were particularly renowned for their crossbowmen. In another direction he could anticipate the sources of that 'thin red line' who were to make the name of 'English' soldiers famous in the wars of the eighteenth and nineteenth centuries, by drawing on the inexhaustible human supplies of Ireland. The siege of Rouen in 1418 was enlivened by the arrival of fifteen hundred barefoot Irishmen, whose weapons consisted of an enormous knife and a bundle of darts. Almost completely undisciplined, they were effective on their nags as a savage softening-up and foraging force, in the same way as the wild Tartar horsemen in the wars of the Turks. For specialists Henry might go even further afield. In particular, for wars involving so much siegework, he, like all sovereigns of Western Europe, was obliged to hire the technical leaders of their day, the gunners and sappers of the German and Italian states. Finally, Henry, like the French King, could have recourse to the feudal levy, an early medieval survival, by which the King could summon all free men to defend him. By the fifteenth century this means of recruitment had been refined, and the King's commissioners could select what men they needed from the assembly of able-bodied and supposedly trained freemen of the shires and towns, but, since the customary terms of service were very short, these amateurs or semi-professionals were normally used only in defence of the kingdom, and in particular in the wars against the Welsh and the Scots. The French, however, although they employed paid captains, the notorious *routiers* and free companies, relied for a major campaign very heavily on undisciplined and largely untrained feudal levies summoned by the *arrière-ban*. Despised by their leaders, such levies could be a real embarrassment in a battle, and in any case their terms of service were too short to sustain a major campaign, as they had to be allowed home at harvest-time. This source of recruitment explains both the normal numerical superiority of French armies and the fact that they usually lost the major battles.

The final and perhaps the most difficult problem facing a king intent on making war abroad was that of materials. An easy, but not complete, solution to this problem is shown by the indentures. This was to leave all commissariat details to the soldiers themselves. As we have seen the soldiers were required to supply their own horses, weapons, clothing and armour. They were also required to supply their own rations, at least for the first few months. Throwing the onus on to the men was a practical solution in a time when departments of state did not exist. It could also be a profitable solution. When the soldiers went to market for their equipment they might well find that the major seller of lances, arrows and bassinets was some agent of the Crown. But this was not the whole solution, for some weapons of war were too bulky and too costly to be provided by individual captains. Such were the great engines of siege warfare, the *marngonel*, *balista* and *trébuchet*. Such too were the artillery, not yet field-guns, but already playing an important part in the reduction of castles. The increasing use of guns in fourteenth- and fifteenth-century warfare was paralleled by a learned and often very lively discussion on the rights and wrongs of this new arm. One view was that it was blasphemy to use such a weapon which imitated God's thunder, another that they were the work of the Devil. In particular there was much discussion on the social iniquity of a weapon whereby a brave man, and one who had spent much hard-earned cash on his defensive armour, could be killed by a coward who would not dare to look him in the face. But soldiers, despite their chivalrous noises, were realists, and English soldiers were more realistic than most, so guns complete with gunstones made their way to France.

It would have been foolish for the King to have relied entirely on his captains to supply their own food and equipment. Even if they were fully equipped before embarkation, there would soon be gaps in supplies which they would be unable to breach in a hostile environment, even with all the possibilities of plunder. And so the King, despite the lack of a proper commissariat, was issuing orders and signing contracts for other things besides the supply of men. His agents in this work were often the Lord Mayor and aldermen in London, or the sheriffs in the counties, who were ordered to find private purveyors who would deliver to the environs of the port of Southampton 'corn, bread, meal, or flour, wine, ale, or beer, fish, flesh, or any victuals, cloth, linen, woollen, or any merchandise, sheets, breeches, doublets, hose, shoes, or any other manner of armour, artillery, or any other stuff'. No doubt the King was, in reality, slightly more specific about his requirements than this quotation implies. Other orders bring a pleasing domesticity into the organisation of war; all supplies of ash had to be used for bows and not for clogs; sheriffs were to take six wing feathers from every goose in their counties to flight the English archers' arrows. Later in Normandy the administration of supplies was to become more efficient, but at the siege of Rouen in 1419 the methods still seem to have been rather *ad hoc*, as evidenced by a letter from the King to the Lord Mayor, who was that year the famous Dick Whittington. 'We have laid the siege afore the city of Rouen – at which siege us needeth greatly refreshing for us and our host – whereof we pray you effectually that in all haste that ye may ye will do arm as many small vessels as ye may goodly with victuals . . . for to come Harfleur, and from thence as far as they may up ye river of Seine to Rouen ward . . .' The aldermen of London satisfied the King's requirements, and as some token of their loyalty and affection sent in addition a gift of wine, ale and beer.

The mention of 'many small vessels' in the King's letter from Rouen brings us to the biggest single problem of a foreign expedition – getting the army and all of its equipment over to France. But, despite the lack of any real royal navy and that domination of the sea which was to be a characteristic of English warfare in later centuries, this problem seems to have been solved successfully in both the fourteenth and fifteenth centuries. MacFarlane comments that 'against a few coastal raids by the French, in which a town or two was burnt, must be set army after army transported and put ashore on the European mainland without disaster, to be brought off later laden with booty and captives', a really remarkable achievement in view of the limitations in naval strength. To put the achievement in some sort of perspective one only has to think of the Spaniards who, century after century, attempted to carve an empire out of the Moslem lands of North Africa, but time and again were foiled by the fact that their fleets were wrecked before the armies had even landed.

The way in which the English provided themselves with transports was quite simple and completely ruthless. Orders were sent out to commissioners in the southern and eastern counties to seize all ships, masters and sailors in the ports, and any other ships that should arrive. The ships and men were not released until the master had made an agreement with the King's commissioner to bring his ship to Southampton. The contract when drawn up was similar to the contract made with soldiers. The sailors were paid in advance and the owners received 3s 6d per ton per quarter for the use of their ship. Foreign ships in English ports were also impressed and in the great armada which eventually sailed were to be found Dutch, Venetian and Genoese ships – the Genoese have always been the greatest of naval mercenaries, and while some of them ferried the English army across the Channel, others were manning the carracks that formed the backbone of the French royal fleet. Finally, before the fifteen hundred or so small ships could make the journey to France, it was normally necessary for the small number of royal ships and their allies to clear the seas for a few days.

Henry v has been credited with the title of founder of the royal navy, and it is certainly true that he was much more conscious of the importance of a navy as a permanent fighting force than any of his predecessors. With new launchings and captures he built up the King's ships to some thirty units of which a large proportion were very large for the age, six being over five hundred tons. The greatest ship of all, the *Grace Dieu*, which was built between 1416 and 1418, was an enormous fourteen hundred tons, but she was unseaworthy from the start and was probably never finished, Henry's pride having outrun his pocket and the skill of his shipbuilders. The main job of this naval force, apart from the protection of the English coastline, was to clear the seas to provide a safe passage for Henry's armies, and it was quickly run down after the conquest of Normandy had provided a second line of defence and a wide choice of ports of disembarkation for reinforcements. Before then the new naval force was very effective, and what naval battles there were in the course of Henry's French wars were normally won by the English, though it was impossible for the navy to protect the coast of England completely from the raids of Breton or Norman pillagers.

Throughout the early months of 1415 the strenuous work of

preparation for war went on. But by late July all was nearly ready, and yet, unknown to Henry, a plot was being planned to undo everything. The King and his brothers were to be assassinated on 1 August, and all who had rebelled in Henry's and his father's reigns were to join in the rebellion, which would expunge for ever the Lancastrian usurpation and place the crown on the head of Edward Mortimer, Earl of March. The nephew of Archbishop Scrope, the son of Hotspur, the Scots, the Welsh and the Lollards all appear to have been involved in the projected rebellion which was led by Richard, Earl of Cambridge, younger brother of Edward, 2nd Duke of York, and thus a cousin of Henry. Although connected by marriage with both the Percies and the Mortimers, he had never given any suspicion of disloyalty before 1415. It is possible that by uniting all the potential elements of opposition to Henry he could have been successful in his aims, but in fact the rebellion was poorly planned and was a complete failure. The attempted invasion of the Scots was a flop, and the centre-piece of the whole rebellion, the Earl of March, revealed all to Henry on the eve of the proposed assassination. Henry acted fast, seized the main conspirators, tried them and condemned them to a traitor's death, and was still able to sail for France twelve days later on the 11 August 1415. The Earl of March was pardoned and fought loyally and well during Henry's wars. But it was the Mortimer–York connection that was ultimately to destroy the Lancastrians, for the grandson of the traitor Earl of Cambridge became Edward IV of England in 1461.

This was the end of that 'scrambling and unquiet time' which for sixteen years had nagged the first two Lancastrian kings in their usurpation of the English Crown. From now until his death the French war dominates both the biography of Henry and the political history of his country. But with the King and most of the nobility abroad it was necessary to protect against a stab in the back. The Scottish border was reinforced and the men stationed there were to give a good account of themselves in repulsing the Scottish invasion of 1417, known as the Foul Raid. The very important job of guardian of England was entrusted to Henry's most trustworthy and competent brother, John, Duke of Bedford, supported by a talented Council which included Bishops Beaufort and Chichele. These men did a good job, for England appears to have remained peaceful and contented during all of Henry's campaigns in France.

At last the King boarded his great ship, the *Trinity*, and hoisted his sail-yard half way up the mast to show his readiness for sailing. A great crowd watched the gay and colourful fleet set sail across the Channel to adventure. Young knights lined the decks to make their last farewells.

> One wore his mistress' garter, one her glove;
> And he a lock of his dear Lady's hair;
> And he had colours, whom he did most love;
> There was not one but did some favour wear;
> And each one took it, on his happy speed,
> To make it famous by some knightly deed.
>
> Michael Drayton (1563–1631), *Ballad of Agincourt.*

5

The Agincourt Campaign 1415

The eve of Henry's great adventure is a good time to consider in more detail the nature of his army. The two main fighting elements were men-at-arms and archers. Men-at-arms were armoured front-line troops and were normally served by a squire and one or two pages. This whole unit was known as a lance. Amongst the men-at-arms the knights formed an élite. By the time of Agincourt the evolution of armour from mail to plate had been completed, and the fully armoured knight or man-at-arms was sheathed from the egg-shaped bassinet on his head to the short pointed sections on his feet entirely in plate armour, each section overlapping the next, and each presenting a glancing surface to his opponent. Padded clothing was worn underneath to help prevent bruising. The weight, though enormous, was well distributed, and it was extremely difficult for an opponent to do damage to the fighting man inside his carapace. It was possible to smash a sledge-hammer on to the best armour from Milan and to do virtually no injury to the man inside. But not everyone could afford such good armour, and more than one knight at Agincourt had his bassinet riven to his jaw. Cheap armour, often indeed made of painted, reinforced leather, could be penetrated by an arrow, and even the best armour had its weak places which might not prove impervious to an English bowman. The greatest danger to an armoured man, however, was falling over. It took two men to lift one knight back on to his feet, once he was down, and in a mêlée there was a real danger of suffocation. An even greater danger was that, once helpless on the ground, his last sight might be his vizor being forced open and the flash of a dagger in the eye.

But while on his feet, and most men-at-arms did fight on their feet at this time, for archers had made the horse too vulnerable for mounted face-to-face fighting, the man-at-arms was a terrifying opponent. By Agincourt, the embroidered surcoats, which used to be worn over armour, had been left aside, so that what strode towards you was a mass of men clad from head to foot in glazed steel, their hips encircled with a jewelled belt from which hung a great sword on the left and a long dagger on the right. The sword with its long grip was wielded chiefly by the right hand, but both hands were often used to give greater force to a descending or sweeping blow. The knight had other weapons too. The lance, shortened for foot-combat, was of little use against good armour, but smashing and felling weapons such as the battle-axe and mace were developing to fill its place. Knight against knight in single combat, there was little to choose between the French and English in strength, equipment or courage.

Where the English had their edge was in their archers. Encouraged to practise at the village butts from childhood, the English longbowmen with their six-foot Welsh bows were still, nearly seventy years after Crécy, unrivalled in Europe. Their protective clothing varied considerably, and in the heat of battle English archers sometimes stripped to the waist as they moved in to the kill with their leaden axes, but a normal outfit was a short-sleeved mail shirt or a jack, a doublet stuffed with tow and reinforced with small plates of steel. On their heads they might wear a cap of wickerwork crossed with iron, and their left wrists were normally protected from their bow-strings by a leather wristlet. The arrows, headed with Sheffield steel, were usually flighted with goose feathers, but sometimes for show they used the feathers of their captains' peacocks. This armament was completed by a hide-covered shield, nearly obsolete for the knights in their plate armour, and a variety of smashing and slashing weapons for the mêlée – swords, mallets, axes, clubs and bill-hooks.

To put these soldiers in the field and to keep them in good condition, an enormous array of tradesmen, specialists and servants was required. As we have seen each man-at-arms had servants who would carry his spare weapons, help to dress him in his armour, assist him in mounting, pick him up if he fell and look after his horses while he fought on foot. Behind the lines were many more. Chaplains and their servants, minstrels, fletchers, stuffers of bassinets, bakers, butlers, trumpeters, fiddlers and physicians – these and many others scrambled on to the transports at Southampton with the fighting men.

Most of these men were so clearly drawn to war by the prospect of gain, even though adventure might provide the spice to gain, that it will be difficult to understand them unless we discuss the practice and

I (*top*) In 1398 Richard II exiled Bolingbroke, but his eldest son Henry remained at Richard's court. In the following year Henry accompanied Richard on his expedition to Ireland. This manuscript painting shows Richard knighting his young cousin in Ireland

II (*above*) Richard II at Conway Castle in 1399. He made for North Wales when he learnt of Bolingbroke's invasion, but found that all support for the Crown had gone. He surrendered at Flint on 19 August

III (*top*) On 3 September 1399, while in the Tower of London, Richard signed a deed of abdication, owning himself insufficient and useless and requesting that his cousin should be a good lord to him

IV (*above*) Bolingbroke, now Henry IV, claims his throne from Parliament. Henry is the tall figure with the black hat at the top of the picture. On one side of the throne sit the bishops and abbots, on the other side the lay lords

v The funeral of Richard II. In December 1413, shortly after Henry v's accession, he took the remains of Richard from Pontefract and had them conveyed to Westminster Abbey. Here they were placed in the magnificent tomb Richard had prepared for himself and his first Queen, Anne of Bohemia

VI Manuscript illustration from the poems of Christine de Pisan, showing her presenting her works to Queen Isabeau of France. Isabeau presided over a luxurious court, apart from her mad husband Charles VI. She surrounded herself with her pet animals and two of them are included in the illustration

VII The Castle of Saumur at harvest time, from the *Très Riches Heures du Duc de Berry*

VIII   The battle of Agincourt, which took place on Friday, 25 October
1415, the feast day of Ss Crispin and Crispinian. From a fifteenth-century
miniature

IX Henry V by an unknown artist

x   John Duke of Bedford, Henry v's second brother, kneeling before St George, from the Bedford Book of Hours. At an early age, John had held command of the Scottish border for his father and had received many of the Percy lands after their revolt. He was the most trusted and talented of Henry's brothers and was left behind to rule England when Henry set off for France laws of the gains of war. The rules of division of spoil were quite clear in theory, though the practice might be more confused. Where there were cases of dissension, fraud or malpractice there were however courts to which contesting parties could bring their case, from the summary judgment of a captain in the field to all the pomp and formality of the Court of Chivalry, the court which tried cases arising out of knightly warfare, presided over by the Constable and the Earl Marshal.

There were two main ways of acquiring the gains of war — plunder and ransom. Once a war was under way there were few legal limits to the scope for plunder, though a commander might make special rules restricting looting, as Henry did in his duchy of Normandy. These rules aside, virtually anyone and anything which was not nailed down was fair game. Permanent structures were the perquisite of the king, but movables, whether belonging to soldiers or civilians, were legitimate prize. As one player in this game remarked, when robbed of his pastime by peace, 'an army on the move often gave a chance of capturing a rich merchant: hardly a day passed without its prize; thus one could afford the superfluities and jollities . . .' Since most plunder was acquired by groups there had to be some rules for its division. In a hierarchical society the basis of such divisions was clear. Shares went according to rank. A mounted man got more than a foot-soldier, who got more than an archer, though even such definite shares could lead to some pretty legal problems. If a foot-soldier captures a horse and fights on it, does he become a mounted soldier?

Ransom had even more complicated rules than plunder, for it was potentially the richest source of gain of all. This fact could have a very serious effect on the successful conduct of a battle. For once a man had captured a valuable prisoner he was of course very loath to let him go again, and indeed the capturer was supposed to protect his prisoner from the dangers of battle. This being so, a battle could well be constantly interrupted by prisoners being led off to some safe place where they could be secure, both from the risk of battle, and, even more, from the rapacity of the capturer's comrades in arms. It was therefore a strong and respected leader who could prevent his battle coming to a sudden end as his captains and men disappeared with their prisoners.

But this was not the only problem. How was one to know who was the legal capturer of a prisoner? In law two things were necessary. The captive had to say 'I yield myself your prisoner'. And the capturer was deemed to be the first man to seize the prisoner's right gauntlet and put his right hand in his. The possibilities of confusion about legal rights in a noisy mêlée are obvious. So, as soon as he could, the capturer made sure of assuring his property in a way more easily defensible in a court of law. Normal practice was to draw up a charter defining the captor's right to the captive, the amount of ransom and its method of payment, and the conditions of captivity, and then to have the document witnessed and signed by a public notary. Even so disputes about ransom were a permanent feature of litigation in the period.

Since chance determined that the gains of war were unlikely to be evenly shared, many soldiers formed syndicates with specific agreements on the basis of which they would share their common booty. Such syndicates were recognised by their captains, and it was attempted to split up jobs such as fighting in the reserve or garrison duty so that, if some men of a syndicate were doing a potentially profitable job, the gains might be shared evenly throughout the company. Contracts between soldiers went even further than this at times. Such was the institution of brothers-in-arms by which two or more soldiers might agree to share not only the gains of war, but also the losses; in other words to pay the ransom of their brother or, if it was too high, to stand hostage while he went home to try to raise it. Not all the gains of war went to the individual soldiers. As befitted their rank, the captains were entitled to a third of the gains of the men of their company. And, as the leader of this band of robbers, the King was entitled to a third of the gains of his captains. The efficient King Henry was most assiduous in collecting his thirds of thirds.

But plunder to be won had to be fought for. So, as the great armada approached the shores of Normandy, it was a relief to find that the initial problem of landing a great army on a hostile shore would be comparatively easy. There was virtually no resistance to Henry's disembarkation at the Clef de Caus on the north side of the Seine estuary, some three miles from the reputedly impregnable walled trading city of Harfleur, now little more than a suburb of the modern port of Le Havre. The beach was rough, with large stones which made movement difficult, and smaller stones fit for slinging, but by 16 August the army and all its stores had been unloaded with virtually no loss.

The next stage was likely to be more difficult. Little progress could be made without first capturing Harfleur, well-protected by its situation and its fortifications, and considered to be the key to Normandy. Set astride a small tributary of the Seine, which provided a constant supply of water, and was dammed by the defenders to flood the surrounding countryside and fill the moats, the city was completely surrounded with massive walls in which twenty-six towers with such delightful names as the Dragon and the Tin Pot were set, some of them 'with narrow chinks and places full of holes through which they might annoy us with their tubes, which we in English call "gunnys" '. Undeterred, Henry entered into that business of siege which was to keep him busy for the rest of his life. His brother Clarence was sent round to the other side of the town to prevent the arrival of a relieving army, while he himself, having laid his great guns within range of the walls, retired to the comparative comfort of a neighbouring hill to watch progress.

Progress was slow. Mining operations were checked by successful countermining and vigorous hand-to-hand fighting underground. The damage done by the King's guns, even the great gun known as the King's Daughter, was repaired in the night by the desperate townsmen. The moat was too wide to use a ram. Efforts to climb the walls were met with showers of sulphur and lime poured into the faces of the grappling English, or by the tipping of great buckets of heated earth and oil. Communications between the King and Clarence were made difficult by the flooded lands, and worst of all the English found the salt-marshes that formed their camp to be a pestilential death trap. Soon men were dying in scores from the bloody flux.

The position of the besieged was no better. Week after week there was no sign of the relieving army which might have been expected to arrive from Paris or Rouen, where the chivalry of France were rather dilatorily assembling to repulse the invader. Stores were running low and time was clearly running out, despite all the heroic efforts of the garrison. On 16 September an English division under the Earl of Huntingdon at last managed to seize one of the main bulwarks of the fortifications. Henry's subsequent summons to surrender having been refused, he decided to storm the town. He kept his guns firing at night to deny the garrison sleep and planned to storm the walls at dawn, but in fact he had already done enough. At midnight the garrison asked to treat, and eventually it was agreed that if they had not been relieved by the following Sunday they would surrender the town, which they duly did.

The actual surrender, as Henry entered into possession of one of the great towns of his duchy, was attended with considerable pomp. Clad

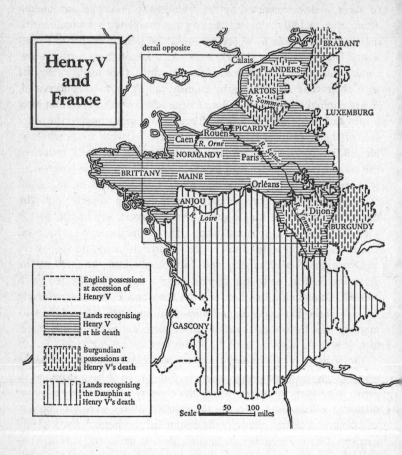

Henry V and France

detail opposite

BRABANT
Calais
FLANDERS
ARTOIS
R. Somme
LUXEMBURG
PICARDY
Rouen
Caen
R. Orne
R. Seine
NORMANDY
Paris
BRITTANY
MAINE
Orléans
ANJOU
R. Loire
Dijon
R. Yonne
BURGUNDY

English possessions at accession of Henry V

Lands recognising Henry V at his death

Burgundian possessions at Henry V's death

Lands recognising the Dauphin at Henry V's death

GASCONY

Scale 0 50 100 miles

in gold, Henry ascended his royal throne which had been placed at the top of the hill opposite the town, and here received the keys of the city from the officers of the garrison, who were dressed in shirts of penitence with ropes about their necks. Well might they have feared their reception from the man who had just proved in the most effective way that he was their lawful Duke, but in fact Harfleur was spared the horrors of a medieval sack and, though the leading prisoners were held for ransom, they were treated with respect. Here as later, Henry was keen to appease the citizens of his duchy.

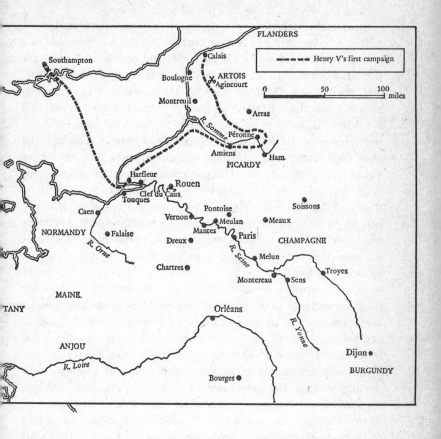

FLANDERS

- - - - Henry V's first campaign

Southampton
Calais
Boulogne
ARTOIS
Agincourt
Montreuil
Arras
R. Somme
Péronne
Amiens
Ham
PICARDY
Harfleur
Rouen
Clef du Caus
Touques
Pontoise
Soissons
Caen
Vernon
Meulan
Meaux
Mantes
Paris
NORMANDY
Falaise
Dreux
R. Orne
Chartres
R. Seine
CHAMPAGNE
Melun
Montereau
Sens
Troyes
MAINE
TANY
Orléans
R. Yonne
ANJOU
Dijon
R. Loire
BURGUNDY
Bourges

0   50   100 miles

His duchy? So far, after five weeks, he had conquered only one town of it, and his army was already sadly reduced by disease. It was now 22 September and he had no wish to campaign in winter. What was he to do? To march on Paris, which may have been his original intention, was unthinkable with his weakened army. Leave a garrison and sail for home? This would have been too humiliating an end to such a glorious expedition, though it was what many of his captains advised. While Henry debated his problem, he sent a challenge to the Dauphin to fight him in single combat, the winner to be the next King of France when

Charles VI died. Hardly surprisingly, the Dauphin, a fat nineteen-year-old who preferred organ music to fighting, ignored this challenge, and it seems unlikely that Henry himself took it very seriously.

By 5 October Henry had made up his mind. At his Council in Harfleur of that date, he is reputed to have remarked that he was possessed of a very great desire of seeing his territories and had decided to march through Normandy to his other secure possession in northern France, the town of Calais. The direct route to Calais was just over one hundred and sixty miles from Harfleur, all through hostile territory, so that this has seemed to many to be an incredibly foolhardy decision. But, as a recent historian has pointed out, to the best of Henry's knowledge the main French army was at Vernon, one hundred and fifty miles from Calais, and, since ignorance of his plans would prevent them setting out before receiving news of his departure, he would have two or three days' start with his better-disciplined and less encumbered army. His only real danger seemed to be the French advance guard in Rouen, and it was worth-while risking an engagement with them for the enormous morale-boosting effect of fearlessly leading an English army through France, as his ancestors had done.

So, on 8 October, Henry led his army, now reduced to about six thousand men, out of the safety of Harfleur. Many of the men were on horseback, but the army's speed was determined by his foot-soldiers and baggage-waggons, so his rate of march of seventeen miles a day to the Somme was not bad going. It was the Somme, however, a river known only too well to the English, which was to turn Henry's well-disciplined and well-organised march to Calais into a desperate struggle for survival. For Henry had gambled on being able to cross the river by the tidal cattle-ford near its mouth, which had been used by Edward III on his way to the field of Crécy. He had sent messages to the Calais garrison to expect him and to keep the ford clear, and he had provided his men with only eight days' rations in order to keep down the bulk of stores to be carried across country. Up to the Somme the going was fairly easy, and the size of his army was sufficient, by threat or skirmish, to prevent much check to his progress from the garrisons holding the crossings on the rivers between Seine and Somme. But six miles from the Somme he took a Gascon prisoner who told him that the ford was staked and defended by the French advance guard under the experienced Marshal Boucicault. To attempt the ford would be suicide, and so Henry set off to the south along the west bank of the river to seek an alternative crossing.

It was now that the troubles of the English army started. Food supplies were getting low, and the resources of the country through which they were passing were not sufficient to feed an army of six thousand, so that the soldiers were reduced to very meagre rations. The men, many of them already weak from the dysentery epidemic at Harfleur, were tired, and their exhaustion was increased by the worsening of the weather, it now being early October, and the general hopelessness of their situation. For, as the English marched through the rain up the west bank of the Somme, they found all the fords staked and guarded, the bridges smashed or defended by great bodies of troops, and every now and then they could see the soldiers of Marshal Boucicault's advance guard, whose numbers were at least equal to their own, shadowing their progress on the opposite side of the river.

When all seemed hopeless, and it appeared as if the English army was doomed to dissolve through famine and disease, as they marched ever onwards into the heart of the hostile country, the geography of the Somme and the general incompetence of the French played into their hands. For between Amiens and Ham, the river, whose lower reaches are comparatively straight, takes a great bend to the east, and so, by cutting straight across the bend, Henry was able to return to the river at a point some two days' march ahead of Boucicault. The French, apparently not so well-informed of the course of one of their major rivers as Henry, were completely surprised, and Henry found the two fords of Béthencourt and Voyennes virtually undefended, though the causeways leading to them across a swamp had been destroyed. A day was spent in tearing down houses to repair the causeways, but by 19 October the whole of the English army had crossed the river.

This was a triumph certainly, but only one which seemed to change the fate of the English army from that of a slow death by famine and disease to a quick one in battle. For between the English and their destination at Calais lay an enormous French army. The main body of the French army, led by the flower of French chivalry, but without the King and the Dauphin who had in the end been left behind, had marched from Vernon across the backs of the English to Amiens, where they had crossed the river a day or two before the English, and were now near Péronne, only some seven miles from the English position. Despite the wise counsels of some, the French noblemen were determined to fight, and on Sunday 20 October, three heralds arrived from the Dukes of Orléans and Bourbon acquainting Henry of their resolution to fight him before he reached Calais.

Where they would do this was not said, but it was understood by the convention of the day that it would be on a field which gave no advantage to either side. For Henry there was no alternative but to carry on, and so he proceeded on his march, now drawing away from the Somme on a more or less direct route for Calais. At this point the French made another of the many disastrous decisions which they were to make in the next few days. Instead of remaining at Péronne, an excellent position with a fortified town and the Somme on their right and a low line of hills on their left, with plenty of room to manoeuvre their vast army in the middle, they proceeded to cut across the English line of advance and to march parallel to and slightly ahead of the English towards Calais. The two armies remained close but not fully aware of each other's positions, because of the broken and hilly nature of the land between them.

No doubt some expert in the French army had advised the leaders that he knew of an even better place to fight the English than Péronne, for on 24 October the English, crossing the river Ternoise at Blangy and climbing the hill opposite, saw, as they approached the village of Maisoncelles, the whole French army little more than a mile away in the plain ahead. They were taking up their positions across the high road to Calais and filled a very large field, 'as with an innumerable host of locusts'. Looking towards the French, Henry could see the field on which he would have to give battle, and no doubt he made plans as he looked.

The field which the French had chosen was almost perfect for the formality of a medieval battle. It was an enormous open field sown with winter corn, about two miles long by one wide. At each end the field was bordered by woods surrounding a village, and it was in these two villages, Maisoncelles on the south and Ruisseauville on the north, that the English and French armies established their headquarters. About halfway down the field there were another two woods enclosing the villages of Agincourt on the west and Tramecourt on the east. These two woods spoiled the natural rectangular shape of the field, causing it to narrow in the middle so that the shortest distance between the trees was only some thousand yards. As Henry took up his position at Maisoncelles the French army was spread out right across the road just to the north of the two woods in the centre of the field. Henry, faced by such a host, made one last attempt to seek terms. He even offered to hand over Harfleur and pay for the damage he had done. But the French were not to be denied their chance now that they had the small English army at their mercy. Revenge for Crécy and for Poitiers was within their grasp. The terms were refused and both sides now knew that they would have to fight next day, Friday, 25 October 1415, the feast day of Saints Crispin and Crispinian.

The emotions in the two camps on the cold, wet eve of the battle have been well-recorded by the chroniclers. The English, well-disciplined and, at Henry's command, quiet except for music and the beat of hammers straightening out spears and armour, must have been terrified at the thought of the vast army of the French outnumbering them by at least three to one. It was all very well for Henry to boast of God's support for his mission to build up his men's morale. 'This people is God's people; he has entrusted them to me today and he can bring down the pride of these Frenchmen who boast of their numbers and strength.' But Henry's men must have felt that they were more than likely to die in the morning and the priests were worked hard as confessions were made, before the exhausted soldiers attempted to get some rest on beds of straw under the almost continuous rain. Only a few hundred yards away, the French nobility and their retainers, confident and noisy, played dice for the privilege of capturing a king, each man as near as possible to his banner, and as far as possible from the hordes of those low station, who were lodged in the adjoining villages. Weapons were checked and repaired, archers waxed their bows, old soldiers comforted young, and no doubt King Henry, too, went round his frightened men, bringing 'a little touch of Harry in the night'.

Henry rose at dawn and heard mass. Disdaining the tactics of his father at Shrewsbury he alone wore the royal surcoat embroidered with the three leopards of England and the three gold fleurs-de-lys of France. With a magnificent crown atop his bassinet he was a marked man amongst his knights in their naked steel. Confident in God's support he arranged his battle. Being so heavily outnumbered he determined to fight between the two woods to his front and thus prevent the French from outflanking and surrounding him. Practically the whole of his effective forces were to hold the thousand yards or so between the woods, leaving only a very small reserve to protect his baggage and horses in the rear. His unmounted men-at-arms were arranged about four deep in three battles, of which he himself commanded the centre, the Duke of York the advance guard on the right, and Lord Camoys the rear-guard on the left. Guarding the flanks of each body of men-at-arms were archers arranged in a wedge formation, and on the extreme wings of the whole line, on the edge of the woods, were much bigger contingents of archers. The archers had been ordered to provide themselves with six-foot stakes sharpened at each end, and these they were told to set in the soft earth towards the French, as a defensive screen.

The French had learned little from the English victories of the fourteenth century, and at Agincourt were to suffer from an attempt to perpetuate 'that unscientific kind of combat which resembled a huge tilting-match'. Their men-at-arms were drawn up in three immense lines of battle, one behind the other, with only the third and rear line mounted. Their leaders, over-confident and divided, had all pushed their way into the front line so as to have the privilege of being the first to strike the English. So massed was their front that there was room for neither their artillery nor their crossbowmen, both of whom were present on the field but played little or no part. The only concession to tactics was two wings of mounted men-at-arms whose task was to break up the bodies of archers on the English flanks.

Having been harangued by their leaders, the armies remained drawn up like this for several hours, each waiting for the other to attack. But Henry was not keen to advance too far, lest he lose his powerful position between the woods. At length, about eleven in the morning, he gave the order 'Banners advance'. After prostrating themselves on the ground, the English cheered, the drums beat and the pipes played as Henry's line moved within bowshot of the French. Now, leaning with their weight into their bows, the English archers fired their first flight whose sting was sufficient to draw on the French cavalry on the flanks, who were unable to reply. Once the French were moving, the archers planted their stakes before them and sent flight after flight of arrows into the mass of French horsemen moving slowly across the muddy cornfield which lay before them. Unable to pass the stakes the cavalry wheeled into the centre of the field, in front of the French front line of dismounted men-at-arms who, weighed down by their armour, were in turn struggling across the mud. The confusion of fallen and terrified horses was already considerable, but the French men-at-arms, heads down against the sun and arrows, pressed on and soon struck the English line. The massive weight of this onslaught of men in full armour forced the English back a spear's length, but then they held, and were joined by the archers who threw away their bows, and flung themselves on the French men-at-arms with axe and mallet. Soon men in the French front line began to fall and it was then that the real slaughter began. For the French, who had already converged towards the centre of the field to get at the English men-at-arms and away from the archers, now found their second line pressing on their backs, so that they had no room to use their lances or even raise their sword arms. Men who went down could never rise again and soon the centre of the field was composed of heaps of armour full of dead or suffocating Frenchmen, on top of which the virtually unarmoured, and sometimes barefoot, English archers scrambled to continue their remorseless killing with leaden mallets and axes. In half an hour the battle was decided.

Seeing the fate of their comrades the French rear line started to move away to the north, and the English, now the masters of the field, began the grisly job of turning over those heaps of armour to sort the living from the dead, and to claim their prisoners. Despite the bloodlust of the English there were still many Frenchmen alive, but most of these were to suffer a cruel fate. For Henry, perceiving movement of troops to his rear and fearing that he might still be surrounded, gave the order that each man should kill his prisoners, these having not yet been stripped of their armour and probably equalling his own army in numbers. His soldiers, their fury now cooled by the thought of so much ransom, refused, whereupon Henry ordered a killing squad of two hundred archers of his own guard to do the dirty work. And so 'all those noblemen of France were there killed in cold blood, and cut in pieces, heads and faces, which was a fearful sight to see'. The only prisoners spared were those of very high rank, whose ransoms were reserved for the King.

Much of the heaviest fighting was around Henry himself, as the French knights who had diced for him the night before struggled to reach him or die. Henry, like a true medieval king, distinguished himself personally in the battle, and in particular saved the life of his brother, Humphrey. The number of Englishmen killed in the battle was very small, the most distinguished victim being the King's corpulent cousin, the Duke of York, who commanded the right and is supposed to have suffocated in his armour when he fell. The French losses were enormous, and the roll of the French nobility who fell begins rhythmically with the Dukes of Alençon, Brabant and Bar, and continues with ninety counts, over fifteen hundred knights and some four or five thousand men-at-arms. Two of the princely leaders of the Armagnac faction, the Dukes of Orléans and Bourbon, were taken prisoner. And, as some sign of the *rapprochement* that had taken place between the parties in the face of the English threat, two brothers of the Duke of Burgundy were amongst the dead. But the Dukes of Burgundy and Brittany themselves were conspicuous by their absence at this terrible disaster of the French nobility. What the total roll of dead at the battle was no one knows, for nobody bothered to count the number of those of low station who died.

The English spent the rest of the day stripping the dead of their armour and other valuables, which they loaded on carts and then, after a night's rest, set off for Calais 'through those heaps of patriotism and blood where sunk the power of the French'. These heaps of patriotism had been further stripped during the night by the local peasantry of both sexes and were now as naked as they were born. The army, with their numbers of prisoners increased a little by raising those from amongst the slain who still breathed, reached Calais three days later, and after suitable celebrations and a fortnight's rest embarked for England.

The news had long preceded them and Bedford had made good use of it by wringing another subsidy out of Parliament before good sense should overcome their patriotic enthusiasm. The citizens of the towns on the roads from Dover, and especially those of London, had exerted themselves to give their royal hero a fitting welcome. The pageant which greeted Henry as he rode from Blackheath into the City incorporated every possible effect of medieval show. Symbolic statues and gaily painted wooden towers, banners, trumpets, tapestries and splendid pavilions, cheering crowds and a chorus of most beautiful virgin girls singing with timbrel and dance this song of congratulation, 'Welcome Henry the Fifte, Kynge of England and of Fraunce'.

The victorious army, suitably rewarded by a grateful King, dispersed to their homes, yeomen archers already rehearsing those increasingly tall stories which would guarantee them free ale for life, young noblemen hot foot to their mistresses, still clutching the garters and gloves, rather soiled by now, with which they had ridden so gaily to war some four months previously. Perhaps we should also think of those noble prisoners, such as the Duke of Orléans, who was to spend the next twenty-five years in captivity, unable to raise the enormous ransom asked for him, an exile that he enlivened by writing lyric poetry, a princely accomplishment shared by another of Henry's captives, the young King of Scots.

6

The Conquest of Normandy 1415–19

Agincourt was an astonishing victory against enormous odds. The battle made Henry's reputation as a fighting King overnight. His prestige in France was such that never again did a French army attempt to engage him in a major battle. In England his success meant that he never had any difficulty in raising men or money to fight in his subsequent campaigns. But Agincourt itself brought him little but fame. At the cost of about a quarter of his army lost by disease he had captured one town and won one battle. Harfleur may have been a useful addition to the English possessions in France, but it was after all but one town in Normandy. Normandy was studded with towns whose defences were as good as those of Harfleur. And if Normandy was the part of France which Henry most ardently desired to conquer, it was still only part of France. Henry laid claim to the whole of France. Was it possible to conquer the whole country in the face of the sort of resistance shown at Harfleur? Many Frenchmen might have died at Agincourt, but there were many more left. While Henry pondered about the future, fresh armies were being raised in France.

One thing was clear; even Henry's most limited ambitions in France could never be achieved if the country was united against him. There was, however, little likelihood of that. Armagnac and Burgundian were still as far apart as ever. So while Henry issued orders for the raising of a new army to invade France, he carried on with his old policy of diplomacy. The great triumph of these years between the two invasions was the treaty of Canterbury signed on 15 August 1416, between Henry and the Holy Roman Emperor Sigismund. Sigismund, who had been lucky to escape with his life after the great Turkish victory at Nicopolis in 1396, had two major ambitions – to close the schism and to pacify

Europe, so that a great Crusade could clear the Turks from Christendom for ever. Henry warmly supported both these ambitions, but his means of pacifying Europe was rather different from that suggested by Sigismund. Instead of making peace with France, he would conquer France. Then there would be peace and he would be available to lead the Crusade against the Turks. During four months of 1416, in which Sigismund and an enormous entourage enjoyed themselves at the expense of the English taxpayers, Henry managed to persuade the Emperor to support his claim to the French Crown. The result was an offensive and defensive alliance which enormously increased Henry's prestige, though in fact no Imperial troops assisted him in his second French campaign. Fresh from this triumph Henry followed the Emperor to Calais and here the two rulers had a secret meeting with the Duke of Burgundy. No one knows what was the outcome of this meeting between what one modern historian has called the three champion double-crossers of the age. But the most that Henry probably obtained from the Duke of Burgundy was once again to ensure that tricky man's neutrality.

Meanwhile Henry's plans for his invasion of France were nearing fulfilment. As in the months before the Agincourt campaign, indentures were made, materials were gathered together and those jewels which had been redeemed were once again handed out to his captains. This time the army was to be even bigger – at least ten thousand fighting men and a correspondingly large body of servants and tradesmen. Once again the muster was to be at Southampton and once again the Duke of Bedford was to be left behind to look after the kingdom in his brother's absence. But this time the objectives were going to be different. In 1417 Henry broke with all the traditions of previous campaigns in the Hundred Years War, for when he set out from Southampton on 30 July, he set out to conquer – to establish permanent English rule. What was it that he intended to conquer?

Although Henry laid claim to the whole of France, or second best, the whole of the former Angevin Empire, or at least the territory promised to England by the treaty of Brétigny in 1360, it is probable that his immediate aims were rather less ambitious, although it is clear that he could rapidly expand his objectives if a real opportunity offered itself. It seems almost certain that his intention when he set sail from Southampton was to conquer Normandy, and from this base to strike at Paris. Even this lesser ambition implied a military imagination and a command of strategical thinking far greater than those of his royal predecessors in the fourteenth century. Where they had envisaged warfare as a series of brilliant raids from the English fief of Gascony in the south-west or from the bridgeheads on the Channel, Henry saw his aim to be the systematic annexation of that province which he passionately and almost obsessively believed to be his own. The *chevauchée* was to give place to conquest, though conquest could and did provide opportunities for new *chevauchées* into parts of France hitherto barely touched by English arms.

Henry's policy for the conquest of Normandy seems fairly clear. If he could, for the time being at any rate, protect himself on his left and right by truces with Burgundy and Brittany, his only likely adversaries in the field would be the forces of the Armagnacs or, as they were now called, the Dauphinists. Since these were being kept very busy fighting the Burgundians in the environs of Paris, he had little need to worry about facing large armies in the field, unless there was some sudden change on the diplomatic scene. What he did have to do was to capture castles and fortified towns, for unless the numerous strongholds protecting ports, crossroads, river crossings and other strategic points were in his hands any conquests which he made were bound to be ephemeral. For a really permanent conquest, four, or possibly five, stages were necessary. First a bridgehead and winter-quarters in Lower Normandy had to be secured. The place finally decided on was the city of Caen. Once Caen was secured, the rest of Lower Normandy could be conquered, and then Upper Normandy across the line of the Seine. But, as all conquerors have discovered, to hold one province it is nearly always necessary to conquer another. To make Normandy secure from the east it was necessary to advance into Picardy and hold the line of the Somme, to reduce the Ile de France and capture the greatest prize of all, Paris. It was no use relying on the Burgundians being good neighbours for ever. And to make Normandy secure from the south it was necessary to conquer Maine and parts of Anjou, Touraine and the Orléanais in order to hold the line of the lower Loire to Orléans. A province bordered by the Loire and the Somme, and including the fortifications of Paris, was a perfectly defensible unit which might well have remained English for a very long time. As it was, the English held Henry's conquests for a generation, but one of the main reasons for their ultimate failure was the inability to produce an army large enough to conquer both in the south and in the east. The Loire was never held, and it is striking that the turning point in the war, inspired by that revival of French national spirit associated with the person of Joan of Arc, was the raising of the English siege of Orléans, the key to the Loire.

Henry's method of conquest was to send troops out ahead to hold the main roads into the area where he was at work, and to prevent the arrival of any relieving armies from the east, Paris or the south. Then, behind this offensive screen, he and his lieutenants could proceed at their leisure to reduce the fortified places in the neighbourhood. Time was on his side and in the whole conquest of Normandy only one town, that of Caen, had to be taken by storm. This policy was a very economical one and Henry lost few men from hostile action during his two-year campaign. Disease, too, that other scourge of medieval armies, was kind to him on this campaign. In this he was extremely fortunate, for all the odds were against the health of an army engaged in siege warfare remaining good, and in fact Henry's luck was to run out on his third campaign, when many of his men succumbed to disease, and he himself incurred his fatal illness.

Before we begin to examine Henry's war of sieges it would be as well to discuss briefly the medieval laws of siege warfare. These were very precise, and belonged to that same code of behaviour sanctioned by law and custom which governed other aspects of warfare, such as ransom. Towns could be taken by storm or treaty. The first stage in a siege was therefore for a herald to go up to the city and demand that the gates be opened to allow his prince or lord to enter. Many castles did just that, and a treaty would be made allowing the garrison to march out. If the garrison refused, however, the siege would begin, and, if successful, the rule was that the besiegers had the right to sack the town completely and kill all its inhabitants without giving quarter. The only people and property that were technically safe were churchmen and churches. Otherwise the successful besieging army had complete licence to loot, burn, rape and kill. The only limit to their bloodlust was the clemency of their commander. Such rules faced garrison commanders with an appalling dilemma: to submit was treason to their own prince; not to submit faced them and their followers with the horrors of sack. The dilemma was in fact too appalling, and a sensible compromise had been evolved. To avoid the charge of treason to their own prince, garrison commanders first made an impressive show of resistance. After a period of time, long or short, depending on the conditions and the personality of the commander, an agreement to cease the siege for an agreed period of time was entered into between the garrison commander and the commander of the besieging forces. During this period everything was left in a state of suspended animation. No supplies were to arrive, no walls to be mended, no trenches to be dug – sometimes indeed an umpire was appointed to see that both sides kept to their bargain. The basis and motivation of these bargains were very sensible. For the agreement was that if within a certain period no relieving force had appeared to give battle to the besiegers, then the castle was to be given up, the garrison could march out with the honours of war and there would be no sack. There would be some reprisals, of course, for the garrison had already offended the prince by refusing to open the gates in the first place, but such reprisals were normally orderly, and consisted mainly of a heavy fine to be levied on the resisting town, and the removal of some of the leading citizens, either as hostages or for ransom. In some cases a few selected citizens and soldiers who had offended the commander of the besiegers would be hanged, and Henry, towards the end of his time in France, was guilty of some very vindictive reprisals of this sort. Whatever the particular form of the reprisals, this sort of agreement was the ultimate outcome in most of the sieges undertaken by Henry and his lieutenants, and since, as we have seen, it was Henry's policy to prevent the arrival of relieving armies, the result was nearly always in his favour.

The towns which had to be taken were in fairly good condition by the middle of 1417, for the Armagnacs had made good use of the twenty months between Agincourt and Henry's second invasion. The castles of Normandy had been repaired and their garrisons strengthened, often with royal troops. But the Armagnacs still suffered from a serious money problem, as they were to continue to do throughout the war. An effort had been made to pacify the countryside, as it was realised that there was little hope of raising taxation from a peasantry unable even to sow their crops as a result of continuous raiding by bandits and free companies. But although the new Constable, the Count of Armagnac, had some success in this direction and in his attempts to improve the discipline and service conditions of his own troops, he was fighting a losing battle, and when the war broke out again France and the French armies reverted once more to that lawlessness and indiscipline to which they had so long been accustomed. Nor, again despite moderate triumphs, was Armagnac any more successful in his attempt to recapture Harfleur by laying siege to the town and blockading the

Seine. For on 15 August 1416, Henry's brother, Bedford, led a strong English fleet which won the battle of the Seine and lifted the siege.

Bedford's success was followed in June 1417 by another naval victory, when an English force under the Earl of Huntingdon won a hard-fought battle against a fleet of twenty-six Genoese and Biscayan ships which were watching the mouth of the Seine. After a three hours' fight Huntingdon captured four of the Genoese carracks and dispersed the rest of the fleet, so that on 30 July, when the English armada at last set sail from Southampton, the Channel was free for its crossing. Henry again kept his destination secret, and his archers were easily able to disperse the small force of horsemen who opposed his landing at Touques, between the modern holiday resorts of Deauville and Trouville, on the south side of the Seine estuary. As we have seen, his primary objective at this stage was the capture of the city of Caen and he set about achieving it with his customary efficiency. While stores were being unloaded, detachments were sent out to secure the fortified places in the neighbourhood of his landing place and to prevent any relieving forces getting out of the garrison of Honfleur. This done, further detachments were sent to hold all the roads leading to Caen, and Henry marched with the rest of his army to invest the city.

Medieval Caen was one of the greatest cities in France. Set in a fertile plain, it was the market town for a normally prosperous agricultural area and also an industrial town of some standing. The city was divided into two by a branch of the river Orne. To the north was the Old Town dominated by a great castle set on a precipitous hill. To the south, on an island formed by the river, was the New Town. The fortifications of the Old and New Towns were completely separate and the only connection between the two was one bridge guarded by the fort of St Pierre. These fortifications were quite new, for Edward III had taken the city by assault in 1346 and given it over to pillage for three days, an unpleasant experience which the citizens were determined should never happen again. At great expense, both parts of the town had therefore been completely surrounded by new walls, which, together with the natural defences of the river, had made Caen into a haven for large numbers of people from the countryside seeking security in a troubled time.

When the citizens of Caen heard of Henry's landing at Touques they immediately began to put their city in order for the expected siege. Food and weapons were brought in from the countryside; jewels, plate and ornaments belonging to private citizens and the many rich churches were lodged for safe keeping in the castle. Welcome reinforcements to the garrison marched in. These soldiers, experienced in the art of siege, saw straightaway where the weakness of Caen lay, for on either side of the city were two abbeys. Although these too had been fortified to provide an additional defence to the city, if ever they should get into the hands of a besieger armed with artillery they would give him an enormous advantage. For they looked right over the walls of the New Town into the heart of the city. At an eve-of-siege council the men of war suggested that the two abbeys and the suburbs of the town should be razed to the ground to prevent their use by the besiegers. But too much of civic pride rested in the abbeys, and the citizens rejected the suggestion. It would be better that they were ruined themselves than commit such sacrilege.

Such was the situation when Clarence, with an advance guard of a thousand knights, marched towards this city of churches, dominated by the majestic hundred-foot keep of its castle. Just in time to extinguish fires which had been lit to raze the suburbs, he was able on his very first night to achieve a success which made the ultimate fall of Caen inevitable. For the French soldiers had ignored the pious decision of the burghers and had begun to mine one of the abbeys preparatory to its destruction. A monk seeing this, and not understanding much of war, is supposed to have crept up to Clarence in the night where he was asleep in his steel armour, on the lawn of a little garden, with a stone under his head. The monk told him what was happening and in tears begged the Duke to come and save his abbey. Clarence and his men were shown a secret way into the abbey and the next morning the people of Caen saw the banner of England flying from its walls. That same day Clarence was able to seize the other abbey with the help of the remainder of the vanguard who had now joined him. Two days later Henry himself with the rest of the army turned up, together with a flotilla loaded with artillery which had managed to force the mouth of the Orne.

Henry and Clarence made the two abbeys their headquarters, while the rest of the army was dispersed under its commanders all round the walls of the city. Soon the town was enveloped by a circle of batteries protected by earthworks. The guns pounded the walls or else, raising their elevation a little, lobbed great iron and marble balls into the city crushing the houses or setting light to them with combustibles.

Meanwhile, lighter guns mounted in the two abbeys could fire down the line of the streets. The French fired back – their guns, though not so big as those of the English, were more accurate and had a faster rate of fire and they did considerable damage, providing some foretaste of that superiority in artillery which was eventually to end the Hundred Years War and drive the English out of France for ever.

As at Harfleur, Henry supplemented his batteries by the use of mining operations, but here too he was frustrated by successful countermining and savage underground fighting. Nevertheless such brave resistance made little difference to the outcome. For the siege of Caen occurred at a date when, for the time being, the advantage lay with the besiegers. The design of fortifications was still in a pre-artillery stage and Henry's guns were making large breaches in the city's walls. After the citizens had rejected with dignity Henry's last summons to surrender, the King decided on a general assault to take place on 4 September, just over a fortnight from the beginning of his bombardment. At dawn, after three masses had been said one after the other, the King's trumpeters gave the signal. The attack was launched simultaneously by all fifteen of the detachments scattered round the city, but the two major efforts were to be led into the New Town by the King from the west and Clarence from the east. The attack of the King turned out to be a very lively fight, and although he was able to capture the Ile de Près, the uninhabited island which formed a wedge between the Old Town and the New, his men were continuously pushed back in their attempts to force the breach that had been made in the walls, and casualties from the showers of missiles thrown down were high.

On the other side of the city the impetuous Clarence, always eager to emulate his brother's glory, was more successful. Throwing his forces across the river on a bridge of boats, he led his men into the breach and was soon over the walls and fighting his way through the streets. While some of his men under the Earl of Warwick seized the fort of St Pierre guarding the bridge between the Old and New Towns, the rest took the Frenchmen defending the opposite wall against Henry from the rear. Attacked from both sides, they had no chance and soon Clarence's men were throwing the defenders over the walls and hauling up King Henry and his men. Henry and Clarence worked their way, street by street, through the New Town and into the Old. Citizens and soldiers fought the English all the way and a final resistance was made in the old market in an attempt to enable the soldiers to get back into the castle. It was here that the worst slaughter occurred. For the open space was packed as people were forced back by the English soldiers. In a last desperate resistance armed men, women and children were cut to pieces.

The sight of a decapitated woman still holding in her arms the child she was feeding is said to have softened Henry's heart and have caused him to check the carnage. He gave the order that there should be no more violence to priests, women or children. This order seems to have been obeyed, which says something for Henry's control over his soldiers, but more than this he would and probably could not do. Caen was delivered up to the pillage of the English soldiers – men were butchered, shops and houses were forced open and their goods seized, until the passions of the excited soldiers were assuaged. It was indeed only the thought of the sack that could inspire men to the suicidal bravery necessary to scale the walls of a beleaguered town in the face of burning sulphur and oil. The horrors of the sack had other effects too. It is significant that Henry did not have to storm another town in his Normandy campaign.

The capture of the town was not the end. The castle remained intact, a small city itself, now full of frightened women and children who had fled there to save themselves from the English fury. So full indeed that the provisions were far too few to enable the garrison to envisage a long siege. Henry moved his headquarters to the north of the city under a pavilion of velvet and silk. Here he supervised the bombardment of the castle, taking care not to do much damage, since he wanted to use it himself once it had surrendered. The garrison's situation was hopeless, and after only a few days they came to terms and were allowed to march out with their arms and horses and a certain amount of cash. Henry moved in and appropriated the treasures which had been placed for security in the keep. As a gesture of gratitude to the real hero of the siege of Caen, much of this was given to his brother, Clarence.

After the fall of Caen, Henry spent a while establishing his administration, while his lieutenants demanded and obtained the surrender of a number of other towns in the neighbourhood. Privileges and tax exemptions were offered to those Normans who acknowledged him as their lawful Duke, an offer which was often accepted. Settlers were invited from London to take the place of those who were dead or refused to submit. Garrison commanders were appointed and the beginnings of the permanent apparatus of government for Normandy were made. But Henry did not stay in Caen for long. He must secure his conquests while the going was good, while the Duke of Burgundy maintained his uneasy truce, and while the memory of Caen was still vivid in the minds of his Norman subjects.

Moving fast he set out to secure the southern frontier of his duchy, leaving the powerful fortress of Falaise unreduced in his rear. With indecent haste town after town submitted to Henry after no more than a token show of resistance. It had become clear that Lower Normandy was going to be abandoned by Paris, and that there was no hope of the arrival of a relieving army. In the circumstances submission and reduced taxation appeared more attractive than resistance and eventual sack. By November Henry had crossed the Norman hills and secured his southern frontier. Truces were made or renewed with Anjou, Maine and Brittany, and Henry turned back towards Caen. Contrary to the normal procedure of medieval warfare he decided to lay siege to Falaise on his way back, despite the lateness of the season.

It was in this great rock fortress that many of the diehard Normans had established themselves to resist Henry in the hope of eventual relief, and the town with its castle on a cliff was stoutly defended. Following his usual procedure Henry surrounded the town with his batteries, made his men comfortable in log huts protected from the winter cold with turf roofs, and proceeded to bombard the town with his great guns. Some of Henry's gun-stones recovered from the moat of Falaise castle measured two feet in diameter and they tore the town to bits. Down came the clock-tower, churches and houses; down too came the spirit of resistance. A month after the beginning of the siege Henry entered the town after the normal preliminaries of surrender. The castle was to hold out another six weeks. The walls were too thick and their base too high up on the cliff for the artillery to be effective. Mining was hopeless in the solid rock, and the garrison was well-provisioned. It was the humble pick that eventually determined the garrison to surrender. Moving up under improvised shields the sappers dug out a shelter for themselves in the foot of the wall, which they proceeded to enlarge. Unable to get at the burrowers, the defenders lowered lighted faggots from the walls to try to smoke them out. Undeterred, the sappers took them off their hooks, extinguished them and continued with their digging. At last, fearful that their castle would topple from its cliff, the garrison surrendered in the middle of February.

By the end of the month the King was back in Caen. Here he inaugurated an ingenious method of sub-contracting the conquest of his duchy. He now held a broad section of Normandy, bordered by the sea and the southern frontier of the duchy, but with unsettled boundaries to the east and west. In order to secure his territories from the borders of Brittany in the west to the Seine in the east, he gave his brothers Gloucester and Clarence lands in these areas, whose enjoyment depended on the submission of the lands in question. So while the King remained in Caen, Gloucester set out west with the Earl of March to force the petty nobility of the Côtentin peninsula into submission, Clarence went east with Salisbury, and other captains, too, were sent to round off the English conquests.

By May Henry was ready to take his war into its next stage, the conquest of Upper Normandy, the lands beyond the Seine. Lower Normandy was now secure, and his communications with England were good, so that he felt sufficiently confident to take the risk that a thrust towards the lands occupied by the Duke of Burgundy would entail. Burgundian was still fighting Armagnac in the environs of Paris, but, since the Parisian mob supported the Burgundians. it was unlikely that the Armagnacs could resist much longer, and when their resistance collapsed it was more than likely that the Duke would turn his attention to the English invasion and break his truce with Henry. What made this even more likely was the fact that Henry's main objective in Upper Normandy, the city of Rouen, was now a Burgundian city. For Rouen, like many other cities in northern France, had thrown out its Armagnac garrison in the winter of 1417, and replaced it with Burgundians.

It was this political situation that determined the people of Rouen to resist the invader with all their power; after the example of Lower Normandy it can only have been the hope of seeing a great Burgundian army marching down the Seine to give battle to Henry which enabled the people of Rouen to endure the horrors of their long siege. In the early fifteenth century Rouen may well have been the second largest city in France, but a city which had suffered very severely both from the ravages of the civil war and from the check to commerce caused by the fighting in Paris and the English blockade of the Seine. These troubles had induced some citizens to move out to the comparative safety of eastern France, but their place had been more than filled by hordes of refugees fleeing from the English terror in the west and the civil war in the south and south-east.

The preparation of Rouen for the arrival of the English was far more complete than that of Caen. Determined not to make the same mistake as their fellow-countrymen, the city council made what must have been an appalling decision. All the suburbs and all other constructions outside the town were to be razed to the ground and the whole of the surrounding countryside laid waste. Churches, abbeys, castles and fine manor houses were pulled down. The magnificent suburbs, as big as towns and more beautiful than the city itself, were burnt to the ground. Trees were cut down and summer-dry pastures went up in flames. The rubble left after destruction was brought into the city to repair the walls. The great city of Rouen was surrounded by a blackened desert. As the English approached, every family in the city was ordered to provide themselves with food for ten months or leave the town. But where could the poor, or even the rich, get food in a wasted province, whose life-line the Seine was blockaded by the English? On the eve of the siege several thousand poor people were thrown out, 'in great sadness', to wander hopelessly in search of food. But very few of the fifty thousand or so left behind had food for six months, let alone ten.

While Rouen made its sad preparations King Henry left his base to join his brother Clarence in the east. Together they completed the conquest of Normandy up to the Seine. But Rouen lies on the east bank of the Seine so, to invest the city completely, it was necessary to get the army across the river. This problem was made more difficult by the fact that the Seine fortresses had been reinforced with Burgundian troops, now released from fighting on the outskirts of Paris by the uprising of the Parisian mob, which had given the city to the Duke of Burgundy. Henry made his effort at Pont de l'Arche, to the south of Rouen. The bridge here was very strongly defended, but Henry was able to outflank the garrison by putting detachments of men across the river on pontoons both sides of the fortress. Pont de l'Arche fell on 20 July and the road was open to Rouen.

By the end of the month Rouen was completely invested. A visit to the old city of Rouen will soon convince the observer that the success of the siege was not a foregone conclusion. The old city was surrounded by five miles of walls set with towers and barbicans, and had a very large defending force inside. It is extremely unlikely that Henry had as many as ten thousand soldiers with which to besiege the city, so a complete investment meant that he had only one fighting man per yard of wall. The city had six gates, behind any of which at any time the defenders could mass for a sudden sortie. A long siege therefore required constant vigilance and attention lest the besiegers be destroyed piecemeal by sorties. Henry in fact never made a serious attempt to storm the city and the defences of Rouen could have kept him at bay for ever, if only there had been enough food. The city's artillery was of exceptional quality and held the English at a distance. Damage was done to the city of course, but the English never got close enough for successful mining and sapping, and the English attempts on the walls were examples of individual bravado rather than mass assaults. Rouen would die from starvation, not from assault, while Henry ensured his own supplies by sending his lieutenants to secure the remaining fortresses of the lower Seine and appealing to the patriotic instincts of the people of London to send him food. While Rouen starved, Henry's army grew. Reinforcements from across the Channel, in particular the contingent of Irishmen mentioned earlier, were joined by men from Lower Normandy as the last remaining castles in the Côtentin peninsula were successfully reduced. Henry's forces were kept busy by continuous sorties by the garrison, and also by the need to capture the one break in his encirclement of the city, the fortress of St Catherine, set on a very steep hill to the south-east of the city. This difficult task was entrusted to Salisbury who only achieved it with considerable loss as his men struggled up the hill into the fire of the defenders.

These incidents apart, the siege of Rouen was just a gamble: a gamble by the defenders that they would be relieved by the army of the Duke of Burgundy or, now that there was a truce between Burgundian and Armagnac, by a united army that would defeat Henry in a decisive pitched battle below their walls: a gamble by Henry that the customary inertia of the government of Charles VI and the indecision of the Duke of Burgundy would continue and force the town to surrender. Months passed, enlivened by incidents such as challenges to single combat between besieged and besieger. But, though the great crowd who cheered their champion on from the walls might have been encouraged by his victory over his English challenger at the first pass, this did little to improve their situation. Messages to the Duke were answered ambiguously. All men's eyes searched the eastern horizon for signs of the great army, but no one came. Henry posted his Irishmen in this direction – colonial troops have always made good cannon-fodder. He even dressed some of his men as Burgundians and ordered them to emerge from the woods and engage in mock combat with his other troops in order to provoke a mass sortie from the garrison. But the people of

Rouen were not fooled.

They were just hungry. After four months nearly all provisions were gone; wheat was long finished, so was beef and mutton, the donkeys and the horses had all been eaten, and the prices of what was left continued to soar. The price lists are evocative. A cat cost ten times as much as a mouse, old leather and shoes were eaten and the people fought for scraps in the street, 'all affection disappeared'. In the first days of December one last terrible attempt to maintain their resistance was made. All the poor women and children, the old and the sick, the useless mouths, were thrust out of the gates. At first the English soldiers, softened by their ravaged appearance, gave them bread, but Henry ordered them to be turned out of the English camp, if necessary at the point of a pike. This harsh order, necessary if his own supplies were to last the winter, condemned the miserable evacuees to a slow death from starvation between the English lines and the walls of the city. The citizens of Rouen made only one concession. When a poor woman was delivered of a child, the baby was passed up into the town by a basket, there baptised and then returned to its mother to die. Meanwhile these dying mothers and children were exhorted to die well by the priests leaning over the walls.

The people of Rouen were not the only people dying of hunger that winter. The roads into Paris, now given up to bandits and the devastation of the mob, were blocked. In the countryside around the capital Burgundian and Armagnac bands were roaming around ravaging the country. At Pontoise, where the main Burgundian army was encamped, supplies were exhausted by late December and the soldiers marched off, not however to the north-west where the Rouennais were still optimistically awaiting them, but to the north-east into the Beauvaisis. The last hope for Rouen had gone and the Burgundian garrison could keep the citizens in control no longer. But even then, so determined were they to get the best terms they could, they did not actually surrender for another three weeks. At last on the 19 January Henry entered the capital city of his duchy, which had made him so welcome. It was a grim homecoming as Henry rode sadly on his black horse through crowds of weakly cheering skeletons to hear mass in the cathedral.

Rouen suffered no sack, though it was condemned to pay an enormous fine for its resistance to its lawful Duke. The fine apart, Henry did all he could to restore the city to something like normality. Food was supplied from his own stores, and citizens were encouraged to submit and once again many did, including the commander of the garrison. Now that the siege was over, they had little love left for the Duke of Burgundy who had quite clearly deserted them when they needed him most. Henry spent two months in Rouen engaged in such administration before he set out to exploit his successes by diplomacy. While he did this his lieutenants extended his conquests towards the line of the Somme, and up the Seine to Mantes.

We will deal with Henry's diplomacy in more detail in the next chapter. It followed the same triangular pattern that it had done for several years, but was now given much greater urgency by the solid nature of Henry's conquests. The main aim of all three parties was to gain the alliance of one of the other two against the third, the enormous cynicism of the whole operation being slightly tempered by a vague feeling on the part of both Burgundian and Armagnac that they really should get together to expel the invader. The net result was that in July a treaty of peace and alliance between Burgundian and Armagnac was signed.

Henry's reaction to this threat was typical. During the negotiations with the Duke of Burgundy Henry's headquarters were at Mantes on the Seine, while Burgundy's were eighteen miles away at Pontoise. Constant to-ing and fro-ing had made Henry's captains familiar with the fortifications of the latter, and on 30 July, the day after the expiration of his truce with the Duke of Burgundy, Henry ordered two detachments under the Gascon mercenary, Gaston de Foix, and the Earl of Huntingdon to make a surprise attack on the Duke's headquarters. Gaston de Foix had no difficulty in getting to his position near the west wall under cover of darkness, but Huntingdon, who was supposed to bar the road from Paris, got lost. As sun-rise approached de Foix determined to try to take the town on his own. Planting their ladders against the wall, his men got into the town almost unopposed, and despite a later rally by the garrison, took the town with little trouble. Pontoise was then given up to pillage and enormous booty was taken.

Henry's surprise move and his new position at the gates of Paris naturally drove Armagnac and Burgundian even closer, and it seems in some ways to have been a rather foolhardy step to take. Captains from both parties took to raiding Normandy, anti-English conspiracies broke out in some of the captured towns, and arrangements were made between the Dauphin and the Duke of Burgundy to meet to implement their July treaty in order to join forces against the English.

But there was too much hate between the two parties for such an alliance. On the appointed day the delegates met on the bridge at Montereau, south-east of Paris. The lack of trust was shown by the arrangements. The bridge was barricaded at both ends and the conference was to be held between ten supporters of each party in an enclosure in the middle. But when the Duke and his attendants passed into the enclosure, the door was locked behind them and they were butchered by Armagnac battle-axes. No one knows for certain if the murder was premeditated, or indeed exactly what happened on the bridge. What is known is that Duke John the Fearless died with a great hole in his skull, and that his son Philip became determined to avenge his death, whatever the consequences for France. For Henry the way to Paris and the Crown of France lay open.

7
The Treaty of Troyes 1420

The English are said to have entered France through the hole in the Duke of Burgundy's skull. In a sense this is true. The murder seemed to be a colossal political mistake, the results of which were hardly likely to be affected by the twelve masses hastily said by the Duke's murderers, as they buried him in his doublet and drawers before the altar in the church of Our Lady at Montereau. It seemed that nothing coud help the English more, nothing could make it more certain that the Burgundians would ally themselves with Henry v to clear France for ever of the murderers' party. But, on the other hand, the murder clarified the issues and, by isolating the party of the Dauphin in the centre and south of France, in the long run forwarded the revival of French national feeling under Charles vii which was eventually to rid France of the English for good.

Before we go on to discuss the diplomatic struggle which led up to the greatest triumph of Henry's reign, the treaty of Troyes, it will be necessary to look a little more carefully at the political scene in France as it had developed during the years of Henry's wars. For it was this political scene that allowed Henry his success. Despite the extremely high quality of the English King's military leadership and strategical thinking, it can hardly be emphasised sufficiently that he could never have done so well had not France been divided. We have seen the hopelessness with which brave garrisons held out at Caen, Rouen, Falaise and other towns awaiting the arrival of relieving armies which never came. Although the failure of such armies to appear was partly a reflection of the enormous prestige which Henry had won at Agincourt, the main reason was of course the civil war.

As we have seen, the civil war was basically a struggle for power between two groups, each of which wished to control the kingdom during the King's increasingly long bouts of madness and to advise the

King when he was sane. For various reasons it seemed unlikely that there could ever be an end to the war unless outside support was brought in. The two parties were too evenly matched for there to be much likelihood of a decisive victory by either of them. And it was also unlikely that they would ever agree for long to peace. There was too much personal hatred and rivalry between the parties, and individual captains had too much of a vested interest in the continuance of the war, their livelihood, to allow it to stop. Each party based its strength on the firm control of different regions of France, and apart from fighting each other and pillaging the countryside, the main objective of each group was to control Paris and the person of the King. Paris was surrounded on the north and east by lands friendly to or belonging to the Duke of Burgundy and his supporters, and on the south and west by the lands of the Armagnacs. Each party maintained fortresses in the immediate vicinity of the capital. But the Burgundians had one built-in advantage: the people of Paris and the other large towns in the north of France were for the most part supporters of the Duke of Burgundy. He posed as the head of the popular party, and the propaganda which he frequently circulated, denouncing the high taxation, extravagance and corruption of the Armagnacs, was often effective amongst the townsfolk, as were his lavish bribes of wine and money.

By 1419 the situation had changed in emphasis. The King was getting old and was mad nearly all the time. Although no one felt like deposing him, and he was much loved by the people as the anointed King and the true heir of St Louis, it was time to think about the succession, especially in view of the ambitions of Henry. The King's heir was of course his eldest son, known as the Dauphin, but what makes French history rather confusing at this period is that the Dauphin was always changing. The children of Charles vi, like himself and his father, were for the most part a weak and degenerate brood, and, unlike the King, they tended to die young. The Dauphin Louis, to whom Henry had sent his challenge to single combat in 1415, had died in the winter of that year. His younger brother, John, had died in April 1417. This left only Charles, the youngest of the King's sons. The future Charles vii was a good example of the physical degeneration of the later Valois. Stunted, knock-kneed, blank-faced, epileptic and suspicious, he was not a prince to arouse much enthusiasm. But in 1417, on the death of his brother, the fifteen-year-old boy was clearly the heir to the throne, and as such was jealously guarded by the Armagnac faction, to whom he was a

28 Henry v in full armour at the battle of Agincourt: a detail from his chantry chapel in Westminster Abbey

The first threat to Henry v's rule came not from the great lords, but from the Lollards inspired by the teaching of John Wyclif. They sought amongst other things to reform the English Church, to strip it of some of its wealth and to challenge the concept of transubstantiation. Henry was adamant in orthodoxy and vigorous in stamping out the rebellion. If the Lollards refused to recant, they were burnt. 29 (*above*) The burning of John Badby, a tailor, for heresy while the King looks on. This woodcut is taken from the sixteenth-century *Foxe's Book of Martyrs*. 30 (*below*) A poor friar preaching outside a church. Wyclif and the friars were at one in attacking corruption in the Church, but Wyclif's more radical teaching lost him their support

31 Wyclif's translation of the Bible into English

32 (*left*) and 33 (*above*) Charles VI, King of France, and his Queen, Isabeau of Bavaria, details of their tomb effigies in the abbey of St Denis

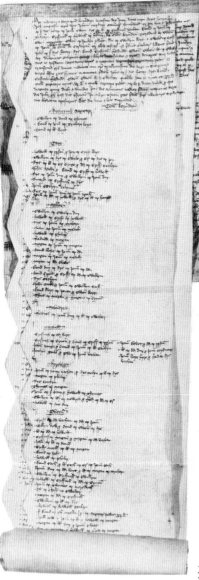

34 (*left*) An indenture of 1413, collecting Welsh archers for the Agincourt campaign

35 (*above*) Rubbings from the monument brasses of Robert and Thomas Swynborne, Mayors of Bordeaux, from Little Horkesley church in Essex. They wear armour and swords of the type used by knights in the Agincourt campaign

36 Marshal Boucicaut kneeling in prayer with his wife, from the Boucicaut Book of Hours. Boucicaut commanded the French forces whose orders were to prevent Henry and the English army from crossing the Somme on their march to Calais

37 (*above, far left*) Defenders of a city making a sortie against the besiegers
38 (*above right*) A sea fight in the Channel. In 1416 and 1417, the English won two naval battles against the French which were invaluable in preparing the way for Henry v's campaigns on land
39 (*left*) A beleaguered city, from a fifteenth-century manuscript, showing the city completely surrounded by the camp of the besiegers
40 (*above*) On 14 August 1416, Sigismund, the Holy Roman Emperor, signed the Treaty of Canterbury with Henry v. Sigismund and his Imperial entourage had spent four months in England being assiduously entertained by Henry and his court. At last he agreed to sign an offensive and defensive alliance with England against France, although he never in fact sent Imperial troops to help Henry in his second campaign in France. This portrait of the Emperor is attributed to Pisanello

41 (*above*) In 1419, the Armagnacs and Burgundians decided to join forces against the English, and their leaders arranged to meet on the bridge at Montereau near Paris. But when John the Fearless and his supporters came on to the bridge, they were set upon and murdered with battle axes. This act ensured that hatred between the Burgundians and the Dauphin would endure for many years and that Henry could gain the French Crown

42 (*left*) Foucquet's portrait of the Dauphin Charles, later to become Charles VII of France

43 (*above left*) Richard Beauchamp, Earl of Warwick, at the French court, taking part in the negotiations for the treaty of Troyes

44 (*above right*) One of the most important articles of the treaty of Troyes: the marriage between Henry v and Katherine of France. On 2 June 1420, the marriage took place in the Cathedral of Troyes

45 (*below*) The treaty of Troyes, between Henry v of England and Charles vi of France. The treaty was ratified in the Cathedral of Troyes on 21 May 1420, on the same day that Henry was betrothed to the French Princess

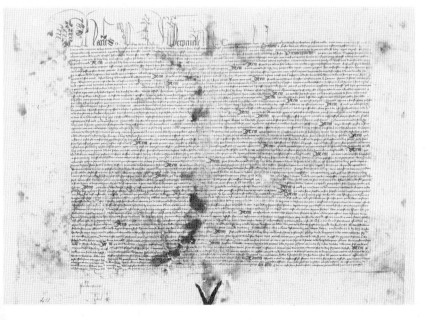

46 (*above left*) The birth of Henry vi, the only child of Henry v and Katherine, at Windsor Castle on 6 December 1421

47 (*above right*) Henry vi became King of England at the age of nine months, in September 1422. He was crowned in Westminster Abbey on 6 November 1429

48 (*left*) The death of Henry v was followed only a few weeks later by that of Charles vi of France, and thus the infant Henry vi became King of France as well. In 1430, Henry was taken over to France by his governors, and eventually crowned in St Denis. He is the only sovereign to have been crowned both in England and France: the supreme achievement of his father's reign

49 (*left*) Tinted drawing showing John Lydgate presenting his poem, *The Pilgrim* to Thomas Montacute, Earl of Salisbury. Montacute was one of Henry v's ablest generals, whom he left to continue the campaigns in France

50 (*right*) Portrait of Richard Beauchamp, Earl of Warwick, from the Rous Roll. Beauchamp bears on his left arm the infant King Henry vi. When Henry v died in August 1422, he entrusted his son to the care of Warwick, who was to be one of his governors and tutors. On his right hand Beauchamp holds a representation of his chantry chapel at St Mary's, Warwick

Richard Beauchamp governed France and Normandy for Henry VI until his death in 1439. His body was then conveyed to Warwick and buried in the chapel built for him in the church of St Mary. This lovely chapel is a gem of fifteenth-century art. 51 (*above*) Detail of the bronze-gilt effigy of Richard Beauchamp. 52 (*left*) A weeper from the side of his tomb. 53 (*right*) A general view of the chapel showing the walls and ceiling. The Beauchamp tomb, with its hearse over the effigy, is in the foreground.

54 The upper part of Henry v's chantry chapel in Westminster Abbey, showing the two octagonal stair turrets and the funeral helm of the King

pawn of immense value.

By 1417 the Armagnacs had need of a princely figurehead, for what had once been very much the party of the princes, the uncles and brother of the King, now had very few princes left. The Dukes of Orléans and Bourbon were prisoners in England, and the Duke of Berry had died without heirs in 1416. The imprisonment of the Dukes in England was not rigorous. They had their coursers, hawks and hounds, their valets, barbers, falconers and chaplains. They slept in state beds specially prepared for them with sheets of Champagne linen with silken fringes. They wrote poetry or formed liaisons with English girls. They had every facility for raising their ransom, but the ransoms never came. Meanwhile the leadership of the Armagnac party tended to get more and more into the hands of tough mercenary captains, especially after the death of the Constable d'Armagnac in 1418. Henceforth men such as the Breton noble captain, Tanneguy du Chatel, the main instigator of the murder of John the Fearless, came to the front. Such men owed everything to the war and had every incentive to continue it. The rewards which they received in jobs and plunder were far greater than anything they could hope to achieve in peace-time, when their lack of princely blood and administrative ability would relegate them to the comparative obscurity from which their military skills had elevated them.

The joker in the French pack was fittingly enough a lady, Isabeau of Bavaria, Queen of France. Back in the 1380s Philip the Bold, Duke of Burgundy, had thought that this good-looking and voluptuous German wench would dominate Charles VI by her animal sensuality and fecundity, and also be an instrument in his hands. The young King certainly fell for the fourteen-year-old girl, though later one of the features of his madness was to be aversion to his Queen. As for Isabeau, there was no doubt about her sensuality and she bore twelve children, but it is doubtful whether she was an instrument in anyone's hands, in the political sense at any rate. Although by no means ignorant of politics, she was very often guided in her policies and attachments by powerful feelings of love or hate, rather than by the good of France or even her own self-interest. If she had ever been a creature of the Duke of Burgundy, she soon swung the other way after the onset of her husband's madness, when she became increasingly intimate with the mad King's debonair and licentious younger brother, Louis of Orléans. After her lover's murder in the Rue Barbette at the hands of assassins hired by his great rival, John the Fearless, she became increasingly anti-Burgundian and pro-Orléanist. For a time, in the reaction following the murder, she enjoyed great power, but later, with the rise of the Count d'Armagnac as leader, she was pushed into the background.

Suffering her hatred for the Count in silence she retired from active political life to the Château de Vincennes where she presided over a picked court of young gallants and ladies, estranged from her mad husband. The luxury and extravagance of her court and the repeated scandals of her private life made the Queen much hated in respectable society, and some of her ladies had a most unpleasant time during the rising of the butcher, Caboche, in 1413. Finally retribution caught up with her. In 1417 the Constable d'Armagnac, who disliked the Queen as much as she disliked him, reported the Queen's latest affair to the King during one of his periods of comparative sanity. The King arrested the forty-six-year-old Queen's young lover, Louis de Boisbourdon, tortured him and had him sewn in a sack and thrown into the Seine. The sack was inscribed 'Laissez passer la justice du roi'. The Queen herself was exiled to Tours, and her treasures seized by the Dauphin and the Constable. In Tours she was kept under strict guard by some very serious-minded gaolers and was restricted to 'a very private establishment'.

The Queen's hatred for Armagnac was now coupled with hatred for her only surviving son. This and the discomfort of her captivity was enough to make her forget her hatred for John the Fearless, in any case doubtless somewhat assuaged ten years after the murder of the Duke of Orléans, ten years in which much water and at least one man had flowed under the bridge. Towards the end of 1417 she wrote to John the Fearless inviting him to rescue her. The Duke sent eight hundred horsemen who released the Queen and brought her to him at Chartres. Henceforth she was a stout supporter of the Burgundian cause and a very useful asset as, despite her scandalous behaviour, she still had considerable authority as the consort of the reigning King and the mother of his children. Now rather fat and gouty, and liable to terrible phobias, particularly of open spaces, she established herself as Regent of France at Troyes. Still frivolous, she soon gathered around herself a new, luxurious court where she presided, surrounded by animals and birds – swans, owls, turtle-doves, cats, dogs, leopards and a special favourite, a monkey dressed in a grey, furred coat with a red collar. This was the lady whom Henry v was to swear to love as a mother.

It will be remembered that while Henry had been engaged in conquering Lower Normandy in the years 1417 and 1418, the attention of most Frenchmen had been more on the fate of Paris than of Caen. John the Fearless, shut out of the capital since the reaction against the butchers' rebellion of 1413, was besieging the city. In May 1418 an ironmonger had opened the Saint-Germain gate and let in the Burgundians. As in 1413, the Duke of Burgundy did nothing as Paris was once again given up to ransack. Bands of wild men led by the butchers and the hangman, Capeluche, roamed the streets searching for Armagnac partisans whom they put to death in various unpleasant ways. In the midst of this confusion the two parties grabbed their puppets. The poor old King, now nearly always mad, deserted by all except a few servants and his devoted mistress, Odette, was led bewildered through the streets and delivered into the hands of the Burgundians. His son was seized by the Armagnac captain, Tanneguy du Chatel, who fled from the city to the Dauphin's own lands south of the Loire. In October the Dauphin proclaimed himself Regent, in defiance of his mother. In Paris the mob continued to run wild, opened the prisons and massacred the Armagnac prisoners with great brutality. Amongst the victims was the Count d'Armagnac, whose naked corpse was left for three days in the streets to be disfigured by his many delighted enemies. After two months of this rampage John the Fearless at last rode into the city, accompanied by the Queen, to be greeted by showers of flowers. It was a Burgundian triumph.

In view of this dismal picture of the contemporary French scene it seems hardly surprising that the attempts at an alliance between Burgundian and Armagnac in early 1419 came to nothing. They hated each other far more than they hated the invader, Henry, and John the Fearless must have been fearless indeed to walk on to the bridge at Montereau. But this should not lead us to think that it was an easy task for Henry to exploit the division in France. For, despite everything, most people in positions of power felt it would be shameful to sell out to the English. Henry had to make the very most of his threatening position at the gates of Paris and the skill of his envoys to get what he wanted.

What was it that Henry wanted? Or perhaps more to the point, what was it that Henry thought he could obtain? Henry v was both realistic and pragmatic, and when it came to the point he modified his demands to what he knew he could get. The bombastic and slightly preposterous demands of 1414 did not seem quite so ridiculous in 1419. Already he had conquered very thoroughly the whole of Normandy and was at the gates of Paris. It was extremely unlikely, in the present political situation, that anyone could take Normandy away from him. And could they stop him conquering the rest of France and seizing the Crown? To many he seemed irresistible. After the breakdown of one piece of negotiation Henry is reputed to have threatened the Duke of Burgundy that he would drive him and Charles VI out of the kingdom. The Duke replied: 'Sire, you are pleased to say so; but before you can drive my lord and me out of his kingdom I make no doubt that you will be heartily tired.' Tired he would be, and no doubt he would rather get what he wanted by diplomacy, but his painstaking and patient conquest in Normandy indicated that tiredness would not deflect him from his ambition.

As befits a man who was both a realist and a dreamer, there was a marked difference between Henry's demands before and after the murder of the Duke of Burgundy. During the siege of Rouen and in the months that followed its successful conclusion, Henry and his diplomatic team, headed by the Earl of Warwick, had several meetings with both Armagnacs and Burgundians. Real bargaining was done – this was not the dream stuff which had preceded Agincourt. Henry's demands were fairly constant. He wanted the hand of the French King's daughter in marriage. If his passions had been aroused by reports of her beauty, they did not overcome his sense of political reality. For her marriage portion was to be enormous – a million gold crowns as dowry and full sovereignty over his recent conquests, and the whole of the territory promised to England by the treaty of Brétigny. In return for this he was prepared to drop his claim to the French Crown. The most elaborate episode in this period of diplomacy was a conference between the English and the Burgundians held at Meulan, between Pontoise and Mantes, in the early summer of 1419. The conference took place in a meadow which was fenced off with an entrance at each end. Elaborate precautions were taken against possible treachery, particularly on the French side of the field. In the middle were three very elegant pavilions, one for the conference and one each for the use of the great persons of each side. All round the field was a canvas city of gaily-coloured tents for the use of lesser men. Here Henry, accompanied by his brothers, Clarence and Gloucester, his uncle Exeter, Archbishop Chichele and his chief negotiator, the courtier knight Richard Beauchamp, Earl of Warwick, met the Dukes of Burgundy and Brittany, Queen Isabeau and her youngest and favourite daughter, Katherine. It was the first time that Henry had seen his future Queen, though it was now about ten years since the size of her marriage portion had first been discussed. She was then eighteen, a tall and beautiful girl, who appears to have done justice to her no doubt flattering portrait. If she was beautiful she owed it to her German mother. The Valois women were on the whole no better-looking than the men, and Katherine's cousins, the daughters of the Duke of Burgundy, were regarded as extremely plain, which can probably be interpreted as downright ugly. So when Henry left the marriage part of his Burgundian alliance to his brother, Bedford, by marrying him to Anne of Burgundy, he definitely had the best of the bargain. But whether he really loved his Queen, as many writers have suggested, is open to question. Certainly on his death-bed he seems to have given little thought to her. Now, at any rate, he behaved in a fitting manner. Henry 'with a most respectful obeisance, saluted the Queen, and then kissed her and her daughter', at which the latter is reported to have blushed in a suitably maidenly fashion. Henry then shook hands with the Duke of Burgundy. But the apparent friendliness of the meeting had no outcome, because, according to the chronicler, Monstrelet, of the exorbitant demands of the King of England in regard to Lady Katherine's portion.

Whether his demands were exorbitant or not, Henry felt prepared to increase them after the murder of John the Fearless. He now said that the only solution acceptable to him was the Crown of France. He wanted a personal union of the two crowns for himself and his heirs. He wished to marry the Princess Katherine, and afterwards to treat King Charles VI and Queen Isabeau as his father and mother. When it was remarked that a few weeks earlier King Henry would have been content with much less, the English delegates replied that this was true but that now things were different, a fact of which the French were only too aware. The fact that things were different led to the eventual acceptance of nearly all Henry's demands, but the negotiations were very complicated and took eight months.

The main reason for the complication was that, although Henry was aiming at an Anglo-Burgundian treaty, he had to deal with three different sets of people: in Dijon with the young Duke Philip and his advisers, in Troyes with the Queen and her advisers, and in Paris with the King's Council. All these three groups were strongly imbued with Burgundian sentiment, but each had a different point of view, and all were much alarmed at the apparent necessity of handing over the Crown of France to the invader.

The easiest to persuade were the Parisians, who as we have seen were strongly anti-Armagnac. The awful decision to deprive the heir to the throne of his rights and let the government of France pass into the hands of a foreign prince was made much easier by the fact that the Dauphin was not only an Armagnac, but also a murderer. Henry on the other hand was pictured as prudent and wise, a lover of God, peace and justice. What is more, this prudent, wise and peace-loving prince was on their doorstep, cutting off their supplies, wrecking their trade and would almost certainly take what he wanted if he was not given it. Above all he seemed to be the only man who could bring peace to the war-torn country.

The young Duke of Burgundy would naturally welcome an Anglo-Burgundian alliance as the instrument of vengeance on the murderers of his father. But it would be wrong to think that he or his advisers were completely dominated by the idea of vengeance. The Burgundian Council carefully considered the pros and cons of the alliance and Henry's bid for the Crown. As the premier peer of France the Duke would clearly be committing a felony against his King if he handed over the Crown to the King of England. This in itself would strengthen the position of the Dauphin. And could either of his future allies, Queen Isabeau or King Henry, be trusted? On the other hand if he did not seize the opportunity of an English alliance, the Dauphin probably would. The Burgundians, like the Parisians, were tired of the war, and so accord with England was decided to be the least evil. On Christmas Day 1419 an alliance was signed between Burgundy and England by which the Duke would help Henry to gain the Crown and the Princess, while both together would fight to destroy the Dauphin, now branded as a murderer and as such unfit to be heir to the Crown of France. To save the Duke of Burgundy from the shame of deposing his own King, Henry agreed that Charles VI should continue to reign during his life-time, but that after his death the Crown and the royal dignity should go to Henry and his heirs. Meanwhile he would bear the title Heir and Regent of France, and would rule the lands which he had conquered in full sovereignty.

The Queen of France was the most difficult person to win over. However much she may have disliked the Dauphin, it was a rather terrible thing she was being asked to do, to disinherit her own son. The story that she publicly stated that the Dauphin was a bastard born of one of her adulterous relationships does not appear in contemporary chronicles. It was probably put about by the English to give more strength to Henry's claim – in view of the Queen's disreputable past, it was an effective piece of propaganda. During the hard years of the 1420s it was a constant worry to the unhappy Dauphin Charles who felt that if he really was a bastard, what was the point of his long struggle to recover his throne? But in fact, far from proclaiming him a bastard, the Queen appears to have been seeking a *rapprochement* with the Dauphin in the winter of 1419–20. Aside from any moral or juridical implications of the proposed treaty, she was very suspicious of Duke Philip's intentions and was also worried that she might lose her present powerful position. Financial and personal pressure finally made up the Queen's mind. To keep the Queen and her court short of money was an effective weapon, for she still kept her extravagant and frivolous way of life. Personal pressure came from Duke Philip's mother, the very competent Duchess Marguerite, who was a countrywoman of the Queen, and from a special envoy sent by Henry. This envoy, Louis de Robesart, was used as a means of circumventing the extremely slow and elaborate methods of normal diplomacy. A native French speaker, brought up in lands belonging to the Queen of France's family, he had acquired English nationality and enjoyed the full confidence of King Henry. We do not know what promises he made to the Queen, but they were effective. On 17 January the Queen issued letters patent condemning the acts of her son and approving those of Philip, and accepting the Anglo-Burgundian alliance.

There was a long delay before the next step in the ratification of the treaty. Throughout this period Henry never relaxed his pressure on Paris, despite renewed truces. Any weakening on his part would almost certainly have led to backsliding on the part of those with whom his envoys were negotiating. But at last, on 8 May 1420, Henry started to make his way to Troyes where the Duke of Burgundy, the King, the Queen and Princess Katherine were already gathered. Henry was accompanied by his brothers and a large force, mainly of archers, for there was a very real danger of attack from the Armagnacs, who still held the line of the Seine and the Yonne, south-east of Paris. The English marched in fighting order close under the eastern walls of Paris, cheered by the citizens on the battlements, who saw at last some hope of a real peace. Minor resistance on the march was brushed away, and finally

Henry arrived at Troyes in Champagne. Here he was met by the Duke of Burgundy, and the two rode into the city together. Later, after the English had been shown their quarters, Henry went to pay his respects to Charles VI. The latter, who was in his malady, did not recognise the English King at first, to everyone's embarrassment, but finally pulled himself together to welcome him. 'Oh, it's you? You're very welcome since it is so! Greet the ladies.' Henry, much relieved, did so and after kissing the Queen and Princess, talked with them for some time before returning to his quarters for the night.

The next day, 21 May, Henry rode to the cathedral to ratify the treaty. Walking down the nave together with Queen Isabeau, Henry mounted to the high altar where the articles of the treaty were read to the assembled multitude of English, Burgundian and French notables. Fittingly Henry sealed the treaty with the seal that had been used at the last great English diplomatic triumph, the treaty of Brétigny of 1360. On the same day Henry was solemnly betrothed to the Princess Katherine. Twelve days of festivities, banquets and gifts were followed by the long awaited wedding, a truly magnificent and colourful affair whose one dark note was the full mourning worn by the young Duke of Burgundy. He may well have reflected, as the marriage bed was blessed, that his loss had been the major cause of Henry's triumph and joy.

So Henry, King of England, became Heir and Regent of France. But it was still a divided France. The treaty and the peace it brought were warmly welcomed in Paris and the north of France, but the south and centre remained loyal to the Dauphin after his disinheritance. The first task of the Anglo-Burgundian alliance was to crush the forces of the Dauphin and bring the whole of the country under the rule of the new Regent. In 1420 this might not have seemed too difficult a task. England and Burgundy together had immensely superior military forces at their disposal, and were led by a man who had shown himself to be a military genius. The Dauphin was young, weak and unsure of himself and his forces were led by mercenary and individualistic captains who disliked working together. Yet in the long run it was the Dauphin who won. By his death in 1461 the English had been driven out.

But Henry was not to know this, and, after only two days of married bliss, he rode out of Troyes with the Duke of Burgundy to continue his campaign. His first objective was to capture the fortresses on the Seine and Yonne still held by the Armagnacs to the south-east of Paris. The three sieges of Sens, Montereau and Melun were very much social occasions – everybody was there, both the Kings and both the Queens, of England and France, and the Duke of Burgundy rode out from Troyes for the siege of Sens. Here there was little resistance, but at Montereau and Melun the non-combatants were kept well away from the battle, though King Henry paid frequent visits to his young Queen. Later at Melun, where the siege lasted four months, they were all brought closer and resided for a month in a house Henry had erected for them close to his tents, and at some distance from the town, so that the cannon would not annoy them. 'Every day, at sunrise and at night-fall, eight or ten clarions, and divers other instruments, played most melodiously for an hour before the King of France's tent.'

All this was in strong contrast to the fighting. At Montereau the Burgundians fought savagely to avenge their late Duke. When the town was captured, John the Fearless's body was dug up, 'but in truth it was a melancholy sight, for he still had on his pourpoint and drawers'. The body was put into a leaden coffin filled with salt and spices and sent to Dijon for ceremonial burial. At Melun there was one of the strongest resistances of the whole war and the length of the siege put a great strain on the Anglo-Burgundian alliance. Quarrels between the allies were common and part of the Burgundian army under the Prince of Orange marched off home. This seemed to be a bad omen for the future of the alliance. The Prince of Orange had been one of several significant absentees, including the Dukes of Savoy and Lorraine, who, although allies or supporters of the Duke of Burgundy, had not ratified the treaty at Troyes. But the Duke of Burgundy stood firm, and took his turn with King Henry and others in the suffocating sport of breaking lances by torchlight in the mines and countermines that were being dug beneath the walls. This strange form of subterranean combat had an interesting sequel, which illustrates in an intriguing way the conventions of late medieval warfare. On one occasion the commander of the garrison, Barbazan, was fighting in the mines with an unknown adversary who, on being challenged to identify himself, revealed that he was the King of England. Barbazan, on learning the name of his adversary, ordered the barriers in the mine to be closed and refused to fight further. Four years later Barbazan, amongst many others, was accused of the murder of John the Fearless. His successful defence against the death penalty was that, having fought one another in single combat, he and the King were brothers-in-arms and therefore the one might not put the other to death – a contention upheld by the heralds in the Court of Chivalry.

Eventually the resistance of the small garrison at Melun broke down before the enormous besieging army, probably the largest army ever under Henry's command. Disease, hunger and the failure of the Dauphin to relieve them led the garrison to surrender on 18 November. The terms were harsher than those of Henry's Norman campaigns. All those in the town, soldiers and civilians, were to be held as prisoners until their ransoms were paid. The fate of twenty Scotsmen who fought with the garrison was even harsher. Henry had arranged for the captive King James of Scotland to be brought from England to the siege. Since the Scotsmen had refused to surrender to him, Henry had them hanged as traitors. Although any method of discouraging tough and experienced Scotsmen from fighting for the Dauphin made good political and military sense, this incident highlights the growing ruthlessness of Henry. There was rather a lot of hanging on this Anglo-Burgundian campaign.

Now that the capital's southern approaches had been secured, it was time for Henry to make his ceremonial entrance into Paris. This displayed the pomp for which the times in general, and Henry in particular, were noted. In front the two Kings rode side by side. They must have made a strong contrast: Henry, at thirty-three, in his prime as a warrior King; Charles, now in his fifties, a poor old madman who had difficulty in sitting his horse. On the left, and a horse's length behind the two Kings, rode the Duke of Burgundy followed by the knights and squires of his household, still all in black. On the right rode Clarence and Bedford, followed by most of the great soldiers of Henry's wars – Exeter, Warwick, Huntingdon and Salisbury. The crowds, lubricated by the free wine running in the fountains, cheered. Priests brought relics for the Kings to kiss. Te Deums were sung. A Burgundian or an Anglo-Burgundian triumph made little difference to the Parisians, who liked to be entertained.

Next day the two Queens arrived and were received with similar enthusiasm. But the show of mutual trust and solidarity soon ended. Henry had already taken the precaution of manning all the fortresses in Paris with English troops and making his brother Clarence Governor of the city. Once the ceremony was over the English and the French parted ways: Henry and Katherine held court in magnificent style at the Louvre; Charles and Isabeau at the Hôtel St Pol were attended by only a few old servants. Poor Isabeau – imprisoned and robbed by her son, often unrecognised or abused by her husband, and now overshadowed by her youngest daughter – what a downcome from her earlier triumphs!

Henry did not stay long in Paris. After splendid Christmas celebrations, Henry, his brothers and his Queen left for Rouen. Here he spent a month putting his Norman territories into order. Then, towards the end of January 1421, after three and a half years away from home, he set out with Queen Katherine and Bedford for England. Clarence was left behind as his personal representative in France. The King's welcome in England was fittingly tumultuous. It is not every king who can return home as Regent and Heir of another kingdom three times as populous as his own. Once again London exerted itself to welcome him. Some of the descriptions of the various displays read as if they must have been kept wrapped up since the ceremonies that followed Agincourt. Here again were the giants, the castles and the lions with rolling eyes, but maybe the wine that flowed in the conduits was now the strong wine of Champagne. And no doubt the virgins who sang a melodious welcome were not the same girls who sang in 1415.

8

The Last Campaign 1421–2

Twice King Henry had returned from France a conqueror. But this time there was a difference; he had brought a Queen with him, much to the relief of the English people who must have been aghast at the thought of a fighting King in his early thirties with no heir. Soon after Henry's return Katherine was crowned, and then went on a royal tour with him round his kingdom. Behind them followed commissioners collecting money for a third campaign. For, despite the efficient administration left in Normandy, despite the welcome of the Parisians, Henry knew that there was still more to do. He had left his brother Clarence and his best general, Salisbury, in France, to continue offensives against the Dauphin. Their tactics must have been dear to the heart of their soldiers. From the southern borders of Normandy they made great raids to the south and south-west bringing back wonderful hauls of booty. It was the tactics of the Black Prince and John of Gaunt all over again, but though profitable, it solved no problems. The Dauphin still had a large army centred on the Loire at Orléans and Tours. He still held strong fortresses to the north and north-east which could threaten Paris or the Duke of Burgundy's capital at Dijon. If the treaty of Troyes was ever to be a reality Henry had to go to France again and win another great victory in open battle. And even when he had done that, he would have several hundred greater and lesser fortresses to reduce before he himself or the son which, unknown to himself, his wife had just conceived, could really be King of France.

Any dreams which Henry may have had were brought up against harsh reality as the royal progress neared Beverley. News was brought that the forces of the Dauphin had won a great victory at Baugé, just north of the Loire between Angers and Tours. Henry's brother, Clarence, always eager for the glory which fell so often to his brother, had struck right down to the Loire and then had had his retreat cut off by a powerful Dauphinist army, strongly reinforced by Scotsmen under the Earls of Buchan and Wigtown. Making no attempt to evade them, not even waiting for the rest of his forces which included nearly all his archers, Clarence marched to the decisive battle he had so long dreamed of. It was truly decisive – Clarence's force was routed. He himself and many of Henry's best soldiers were killed, the Earls of Huntingdon and Somerset were prisoners, and the prestige of English arms won at Agincourt was lost. Popular opinion in England said that the battle was lost because the invincible English archers were not there. And certainly when the skilful Salisbury arrived with the archers, he was able to extricate what remained of the army from its vulnerable position. And in that summer of 1421 he was to lead one of the most successful of all his raids. He reported to Henry that he had just 'come home from a journey which I had made into Anjou and Maine whereat I had assembled with the great part of the captains of your land; and blessed be God we sped right well'. Everyone was happy because they brought back 'the fairest and greatest prey of beasts that ever they saw'.

But Henry was not happy. The disaster of Baugé led to a treaty between the Dauphin and the Duke of Brittany in May, and soon Salisbury was having to operate on the western borders of Normandy to drive off Breton raids. The Burgundian alliance was strained too. In Picardy Jacques d'Harcourt, a former Burgundian supporter who had rejected the treaty of Troyes, was raiding and recapturing castles. The Duke himself was much aggrieved at the welcome given in England to his erring niece, Jacqueline of Hainault, who had deserted her Burgundian husband. This lady was eventually to strain the Burgundian alliance to breaking-point when she obtained a divorce from the false Pope, Benedict XIII, and married Henry's younger brother, Humphrey of Gloucester. But matters were bad enough already when Henry set sail on 10 June 1421 on his third campaign.

Henry landed at Calais with four thousand fresh men. He met the Duke at Montreuil and no doubt patched up relations with him. For the moment it was agreed that two things were vital, to staunch the Dauphinist counter-offensive and to quell the rebellion in Picardy – Anglo-Burgundian France was on the defensive. Within a year Henry had restored English prestige and the *status quo*. But the brilliance of his last campaign, during part of which he was already sickening, only underlines the hopelessness of his task. He relieved the Dauphinist siege of Chartres, captured Dreux, whose garrison had been raiding to the west of Paris, marched south seeking the Dauphin's army and raided under the walls of Orléans. Then he marched north-east and besieged and eventually captured Meaux, whose garrison had been raiding Paris on the east. Military writers praise his campaign, particularly the siege of Meaux which has been acclaimed as his masterpiece, but what had been achieved? A few more formerly Dauphinist cities now had English or Burgundian garrisons. A few more prisoners had been captured and no doubt sooner or later would pay their ransoms. A few more men had been hanged 'pour encourager les autres'. Paris had been relieved of pressure. But the Dauphin's army was still strong beyond the Loire and resisted all attempts to lure them into battle. Baugé gave Henry's opponents confidence, but it did not make them foolhardy enough to risk another Agincourt. Meanwhile it took the most brilliant soldier of his day seven months to capture Meaux, with all the skills that he and his men had accumulated in four years of constant siege warfare. How many months would it take to advance to the line of the Loire and capture such strongholds as Orléans, Tours and Angers? And where was the Loire? From Caen to Tours is 135 miles as the crow flies. From Tours to Nîmes, recently captured by the Dauphin, is over three hundred miles – three hundred miles of Dauphinist territory. Admittedly as the English went further south, they would be able to operate on three fronts, from Gascony, the Loire and from Duke Philip's own duchy of Burgundy. No doubt Gascon, Languedocien and Provençal captains would turn their coats at the first sign of a complete collapse of the Dauphin. But it was still a daunting prospect. As Henry left the successful siege of Meaux to meet his Queen at Vincennes, did he really believe that the baby she had left behind at Windsor would ever be greeted as King in Bourges, the capital of the Dauphinist territories, or Lyons, the greatest city in southern France, which had never wavered in its support for Orléanist, Armagnac or Dauphin?

Perhaps it is as well that Henry could not foresee the future. The baby that Queen Katherine described to him was to have nearly as miserable a reign as the poor mad Valois King, once again left almost alone as Henry and Katherine held great state in the Louvre. He too was to become mad. He too was to see his kingdom fought over by two great factions. And Henry's Queen was to marry Owen Tudor, an officer in her household, one of those Welsh country-gentlemen who had been strong in support of Glendower, and to become the grandmother of the Henry Tudor who ended this faction fight at Bosworth Field. But, for the moment, as Henry discussed future operations with the Duke of Burgundy, he must have been more worried about himself. Victory in France depended so much on his own personal qualities, and he was sick. In late 1421 a doctor had been sent out from England to attend him at the siege of Meaux. By the summer of the next year he was really ill, though he tried hard to fight off his illness. In July it seemed that there was a real chance of fighting a major battle against the Dauphin, who was besieging Cosne, a Burgundian stronghold on the upper Loire. The Dauphin and Duke Philip had even agreed a date for the battle, though in fact it never took place. Henry tried to ride to lead the combined armies, but found this impossible. The once proud warrior could no longer sit on a horse – he was carried in a litter as far south as Corbeil on the Seine, near to his previous triumph at Melun. Here, after some improvement, he once again relapsed and was rowed back down the Seine to the outskirts of Paris. One last effort to ride a horse ended in ignominy and he was carried in a litter to his favourite French castle of Vincennes, where he died three weeks later on 31 August 1422. No one knows for certain what the nature of King Henry's illness was. It seems probable that it was that scourge of medieval soldiers, dysentery – the bloody flux – aggravated by inflammation of the bowel. He remained capable to the end, and during the last three weeks he made calm and deliberate arrangements for the future of his two kingdoms. His brother Bedford was to be Regent of France and Governor of Normandy; his brother Gloucester was to be Regent of England, subordinate to Bedford; his uncles, Bishop Beaufort and the Duke of Exeter, his friend Richard Beauchamp, Earl of Warwick, and Bedford were to be the tutors and governors of the infant Henry VI. No place in the government or the upbringing of the child was found for his widow, Queen Katherine – England and France were to be ruled by Englishmen. As for the war, he pressed those gathered round his deathbed to continue fighting until all France had accepted the treaty of Troyes, and to maintain the Burgundian alliance at all costs. But maybe at last he saw the hopelessness of ever achieving this policy, for he also said that no treaty should ever be made with the Dauphin which did not ensure that Normandy remained in English hands. And maybe it was really only Normandy that he wanted – beautiful, fertile Normandy that had been lost two hundred years before, Normandy that he had conquered so brilliantly – his own duchy – the one part of northern France that was really and truly in English hands.

The funeral of Henry v was perhaps the most magnificent of all his royal processions. The body was dismembered and the flesh separated from the bones by boiling. Flesh and bones were then placed in a leaden casket with a great quantity of spices – a sensible preparation, since it was to be two months before he was buried. In great state the body was carried to St Denis, the burial place of the kings of France and thence to Rouen, his own capital, where Queen Katherine joined the procession. Then the slow procession moved to Abbeville, Boulogne and Calais. The coffin was carried on a cart drawn by four great black horses, and on a bed above the coffin was a more than life-size effigy of the King in royal robes. Bedford, who was in charge of the proceedings, was determined that the French and especially the Normans would long remember the funeral of Henry the Conqueror. Everywhere the bells tolled and relays of priests chanted continuously the office of the dead. Once across the Channel the procession was equally magnificent, until at last the King was buried in the Abbey church at Westminster, with more ceremony than had been seen at a royal funeral in England for two hundred years.

Henry the Conqueror was dead. The most celebrated of England's late medieval kings has had an extraordinary press over the years. Even the Armagnac chroniclers admired him. In some ways it was lucky for his reputation that he reigned for only nine years and died at the age of thirty-five, for few men can win for ever. And in his last years various unpleasant characteristics of ruthlessness and cruelty were coming to the fore. But for the most part the mask he put on at his accession was effective. As his friend Richard Beauchamp played the part of an Arthurian knight until he was one, so did Henry play the part of a medieval hero-king. He was the last to do so. Half a century later Caxton deplored the decline of chivalry. 'What do ye now but go to the bagnios and play at dice? Leave this, leave it and read the noble volumes of the Holy Grail. And also behold that victorious and noble king, Harry the Fifth.' But he was too late – Henry's was the last great medieval adventure.

In the new world that was dawning Henry's kind of foreign policy was out of date. For that reason his pursuit of dynastic knight-errantry has been castigated by many modern historians. He is blamed for dooming

England to a generation of warfare and expense incurred in a futile attempt to maintain his conquests in France. He is blamed for marrying the daughter of a madman. He is even blamed for dying young. Maybe the modern writers are correct. Maybe it is wrong to believe oneself the rightful King of another country and lead one's subjects to prove that right by force. Maybe it would have been better to stay at home and forward the arts of peace. But it would surely have been a strange thing for a man brought up to fight to do. Henry, like anybody else, was the product of his times, and in his times warfare was endemic. That he was loyal, just and merciful as well as a soldier of genius meant that the men of his time admired and respected him. We may suspect that he was a successful showman as well as a successful soldier, but how can we ever be sure? If he was a hypocrite he was a very successful one, for he has succeeded in fooling not only his contemporaries but also our greatest playwright and many modern historians. So, as the dead march plays, let us join his brother Bedford in praising 'King Henry the Fifth, too famous to live long!'

HOUSE OF PLANTAGENET

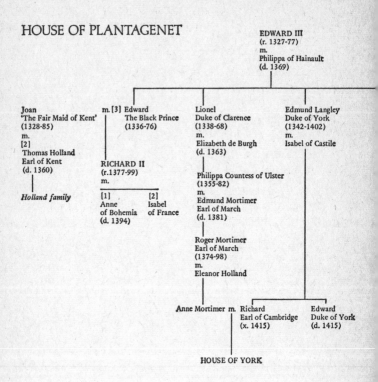

EDWARD III
(r. 1327-77)
m.
Philippa of Hainault
(d. 1369)

Joan
'The Fair Maid of Kent'
(1328-85)
m.
[2]
Thomas Holland
Earl of Kent
(d. 1360)

Holland family

m. [3] Edward
The Black Prince
(1336-76)

RICHARD II
(r.1377-99)
m.

[1]
Anne
of Bohemia
(d. 1394)

[2]
Isabel
of France

Lionel
Duke of Clarence
(1338-68)
m.
Elizabeth de Burgh
(d. 1363)

Philippa Countess of Ulster
(1355-82)
m.
Edmund Mortimer
Earl of March
(d. 1381)

Roger Mortimer
Earl of March
(1374-98)
m.
Eleanor Holland

Edmund Langley
Duke of York
(1342-1402)
m.
Isabel of Castile

Anne Mortimer m. Richard
Earl of Cambridge
(x. 1415)

Edward
Duke of York
(d. 1415)

HOUSE OF YORK

Key: Kings of England EDWARD III

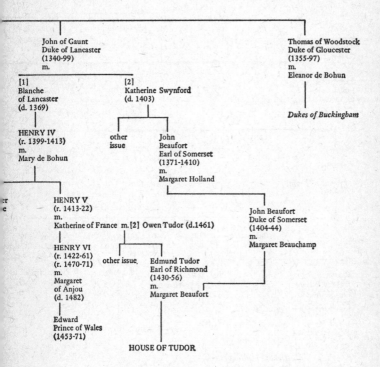

John of Gaunt
Duke of Lancaster
(1340-99)
m.

Thomas of Woodstock
Duke of Gloucester
(1355-97)
m.
Eleanor de Bohun

Dukes of Buckingham

[1]
Blanche
of Lancaster
(d. 1369)

[2]
Katherine Swynford
(d. 1403)

HENRY IV
(r. 1399-1413)
m.
Mary de Bohun

other
issue

John
Beaufort
Earl of Somerset
(1371-1410)
m.
Margaret Holland

HENRY V
(r. 1413-22)
m.
Katherine of France m. [2] Owen Tudor (d.1461)

John Beaufort
Duke of Somerset
(1404-44)
m.
Margaret Beauchamp

HENRY VI
(r. 1422-61)
(r. 1470-71)
m.
Margaret
of Anjou
(d. 1482)

other issue

Edmund Tudor
Earl of Richmond
(1430-56)
m.
Margaret Beaufort

Edward
Prince of Wales
(1453-71)

HOUSE OF TUDOR

HOUSE OF VALOIS

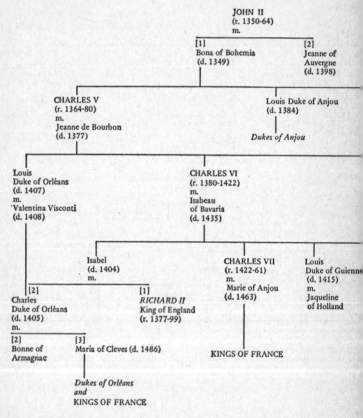

JOHN II
(r. 1350-64)
m.

[1]
Bona of Bohemia
(d. 1349)

[2]
Jeanne of
Auvergne
(d. 1398)

CHARLES V
(r. 1364-80)
m.
Jeanne de Bourbon
(d. 1377)

Louis Duke of Anjou
(d. 1384)

Dukes of Anjou

Louis
Duke of Orléans
(d. 1407)
m.
Valentina Visconti
(d. 1408)

CHARLES VI
(r. 1380-1422)
m.
Isabeau
of Bavaria
(d. 1435)

Isabel
(d. 1404)
m.

CHARLES VII
(r. 1422-61)
m.
Marie of Anjou
(d. 1463)

Louis
Duke of Guienne
(d. 1415)
m.
Jaqueline
of Holland

[2]
Charles
Duke of Orléans
(d. 1405)
m.

[1]
RICHARD II
King of England
(r. 1377-99)

[2]
Bonne of
Armagnac

[3]
Maria of Cleves (d. 1486)

KINGS OF FRANCE

Dukes of Orléans
and
KINGS OF FRANCE

Key: Kings of France JOHN II

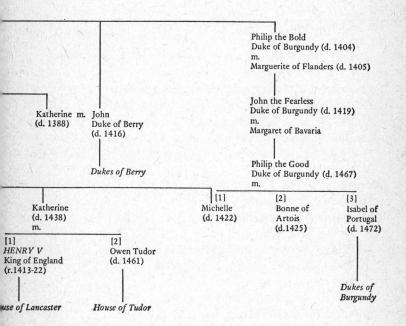

Philip the Bold
Duke of Burgundy (d. 1404)
m.
Marguerite of Flanders (d. 1405)

Katherine m. John
(d. 1388)   Duke of Berry
           (d. 1416)

John the Fearless
Duke of Burgundy (d. 1419)
m.
Margaret of Bavaria

Dukes of Berry

Philip the Good
Duke of Burgundy (d. 1467)
m.

Katherine
(d. 1438)
m.

[1]
Michelle
(d. 1422)

[2]
Bonne of
Artois
(d.1425)

[3]
Isabel of
Portugal
(d. 1472)

[1]
HENRY V
King of England
(r.1413-22)

[2]
Owen Tudor
(d. 1461)

use of Lancaster   *House of Tudor*

*Dukes of
Burgundy*

SELECT BIBLIOGRAPHY

The fullest account of the whole period, and a mine of facts, is the lifetime work of J. H. Wylie:

    History of England under Henry the Fourth, 4 vols (1884–98)

    The Reign of Henry V, 3 vols (1914–29)

The standard textbook is the Oxford History of England:

    E. F. Jacob, *The Fifteenth Century 1399–1485* (1961)

and there are some interesting essays on the fifteenth century as a whole, including 'Fifteenth-century history in Shakespeare's plays' in:

    C. L. Kingsford, *Prejudice and Promise in Fifteenth Century England* (1925)

The most modern biography of Henry v is:

    Harold F. Hutchison, *Henry V* (1967)

Recent biographies of other important figures include:

    A. Steel, *Richard II* (1941)

    J. L. Kirby, *Henry IV of England* (1970)

    Glanmor Williams, *Owen Glendower* (1966)

    Richard Vaughan, *John the Fearless* (1966)

For the events of the Anglo-French Wars see:

    E. Perroy, *The Hundred Years' War* (1951)

    A. H. Burne, *The Agincourt War* (1956)

    R. A. Newhall, *The English Conquest of Normandy, 1416–24* (1924)

and a fascinating collection of contemporary accounts and documents:

    Sir N. Harris Nicholas, *History of the Battle of Agincourt* (1827) (facsimile ed. 1970)

For the organisation of war during this period:

    M. H. Keen, *Laws of War in the Late Middle Ages* (1965)

    Michael Powicke, *Military Obligation in Medieval England* (1962)

    H. J. Hewitt, *Organization of War under Edward III*

    R. A. Newhall, *Muster and Review* (1940)

For social and intellectual history the following are very useful:

E. Rickert, *Chaucer's World* (1948), extracts from contemporary books, etc.

A. L. Poole (ed.), *Medieval England*, 2 vols (1958) – essays on military architecture, arms and armour, recreation, costume, etc.

Gervase Mathew, *The Court of Richard II* (1968)

K. B. MacFarlane, *John Wycliffe and the beginnings of English Nonconformity* (1952)

INDEX